THE
DAMAGE DONE

TWELVE YEARS OF HELL IN A BANGKOK PRISON

WARREN FELLOWS

MAINSTREAM
PUBLISHING

*This is dedicated to my mum and to the
memory of Paul Hayward.*

First published in Great Britain in 1998 by
MAINSTREAM PUBLISHING COMPANY (EDINBURGH) LTD
7 Albany Street
Edinburgh EH1 3UG

This edition 1999
Reprinted 1999, 2000, 2001, **2002**

ISBN 1 84018 275 X

First published in 1997 by
Pan Macmillan Australia Pty Limited
St Martins Tower, 31 Market Street, Sydney

A catalogue record for this book is available from the British Library

Printed in Great Britain by Cox & Wyman Ltd

CONTENTS

PROLOGUE

I AM GOING to tell you about the worst thing that ever happened to me.

I don't really want to tell you, because it's too terrible for me to recall, but I have to tell you. It's important that you know, and I have to get it out of my heart.

This thing went on for eleven and a half years. Think about that. Think of the most wretched day of your life – maybe it's when somebody you loved died, or when you were badly hurt in an accident, or a day when you were so terrified you could scarcely bare it. Imagine 4,000 of those days, together in one big chunk, and you're getting close.

I do not tell this story to bring pity on myself. I know that many people hate me for what I did and would believe that I deserved whatever I got. I can only ask those people to keep reading. If, at the end of my story, you still believe that anyone could deserve the horrors that I saw, then you, too, are a criminal. A vengeful and sadistic one. Maybe you just haven't been caught yet.

I'll tell you of something I saw in a prison called Bang Kwang, nine years into my imprisonment in Thailand. This isn't an isolated incident – it's one of many – but it is one that stays in my head and plays like a short horror movie, over and over.

I was awakened late one night by the screaming of a young French prisoner in the cell next door. The sound of his scream was excruciating. It wasn't just a scream of pain, but of madness too. It was the sort of sound you would never want to hear coming from a human being. I'll never forget it. For hours and hours he screamed, until I and a friend called David, who was in a cell opposite, began screaming back, begging him to tell us what was wrong. It became obvious that whatever was torturing him was so overwhelming that he couldn't hear us at all. He was lost in his own pain.

Eventually, David and I began shouting for the guard. We knew that the hospital staff, who didn't care too much at the best of times, wouldn't be interested at this hour. So we pleaded with the guard to let us into the Frenchman's cell to see what was wrong. David had served in the US army, knew a fair amount of first aid and thought he might be able to help. Luckily, we had a good guard this night, and he agreed.

When we entered the Frenchman's cell, he was alone, curled into a ball, facing the corner. His screams didn't stop for the whole time we were there – he seemed totally oblivious of our presence. As soon as we turned him over, we saw what was wrong. On his neck, just below the ear, was an enormous lump, about the size of an avocado. As we looked at this lump, it appeared to be moving.

David seemed to know what was going on and dashed back to our cell to get a razor blade (keeping razors was illegal in Bang Kwang, but the guard, who was now as concerned as we were, turned a blind eye this time). David told us to hold the Frenchman down, as he was going to lance the lump with the razor. As soon as the blade sliced the skin, the wound opened up like a new flower. And out of the gash in the Frenchman's neck spilled hundreds of tiny, worm-like creatures, wriggling and oozing out like spaghetti. It was appalling, a dreadful dream, only real and right before my eyes, happening to a human being. According to the hospital staff who examined him later, a cockroach had crawled into his ear, burrowed through to his neck and laid its eggs. A man who, somewhere, had a mother and a father, family and friends, had been left to become a living nest for maggots. And when I remember the grotesque sound of his screams, I'm certain he knew what was happening to him.

This little scene didn't have a staggering impact on me at the time. It should have, but it didn't. Such visions marked my days like the chimes of a clock. One ill moment means a lot on its own. Place it in the middle of a million other ills and it means nothing.

I remember seeing a young American, who'd just arrived in the prison, crying one night and I said to him, 'What's the matter?' Looking back, it was a ridiculous question. Everything was the matter. But I'd lost touch with how sick our circumstances were, and I no longer had any recollection of what it was to live like a normal human being.

Today, when I walk around, I sometimes find myself wondering if the whole thing, my whole experience there, really happened at all. It seems so unreal. At other times, it feels as if this new life is far away – even though I'm surrounded by it – and the one I lived through in those dungeons in Bangkok is my true life, still out there, waiting for me to return. It seems impossible that both worlds could exist at the same time. They're natural enemies. Surely one would conquer the other.

CHAPTER 1

CHANCE

MY FATHER RODE the winner of the Melbourne Cup in 1949. Bill Fellows and Foxzami strode home easily, a few lengths ahead of the field. Things looked good for the family, which at that point consisted of my father, my mother, four-year-old Gary and two-year-old Gail. I was to follow in 1953. But the future of the Fellows family began to collapse before I had even entered it. Six months after my father's victory, Gail died of a bowel complication. My father never really recovered. He lost interest in competing and, by all accounts, seemed to surrender his spirit. I remember him as a fairly happy person, but I was always aware of a certain sorrowfulness underneath, a discomfort from which he didn't seem to want to escape.

Nevertheless, he continued working with racehorses and became a very sought-after trainer. Naturally, I spent a lot of my youth around him, at the training sessions and the racetrack. I used to love going to the track with my father. I knew he was an important figure and I enjoyed being a part of the action.

It was at the track where I developed my interest in punting. Like every punter, I loved winning, but I also loved the thrill that came from knowing that I was always close to a catastrophic loss.

This compulsion continued until, 30 years after my father, my picture appeared in the papers too. But I'm not raising a trophy or being congratulated by anyone – I am cowering behind my own hand as 8.5 kilograms of heroin are displayed on a table in front of me.

The story of how I came to be in this picture is a labyrinth of chance meetings and bad decisions. As I have told you, I have always been drawn to a game where a degree of chance is involved. But I believe my turning point, the crossroads where I veered towards my fate, came to me while I was working in a bar in Wynyard, deep in Sydney's central business district. It was here that I met Richard, a guy who drank in the bar who also seemed to be doing a good deal of SP bookmaking work.

One night, he called me over and asked me a favour – he said he was holding a bit too much money for comfort, and asked if I would please slip around to the TAB to place $500 for him. I was not alarmed at this – through my experience at racetracks, bookmakers were a shady breed who rarely did harm to anyone except themselves, or those who owed them money. I began to run these errands for him regularly. My employer didn't seem to mind. He'd seen his share of murky behaviour and accepted it as life in public bars.

After a while, Richard and I became good friends. We drank together after hours and got on well. We also shared the same birthdate: 13 September.

One night at the bar, Richard asked me if I was interested in a bit of adventure. He said he had a sensational contact who could get us some hashish very cheaply. All we had to do, he said, was travel to India and return to sell the hashish for a sizeable profit.

Until this point, at the age of 21, drugs had played no part in my life. I honestly had no idea what most drugs looked like – they were indulged in by people far from my world and I just wasn't interested. I had heard a few stories during my time as an apprentice hairdresser, working in the toffee Sydney suburb of Double Bay. Just your usual high-flying tales of indulgence. The question of where these drugs came from had never occurred to me, and the idea that I was close to the traffic, or capable of entering it, or that drugs would change the shape of my life forever, was just unthinkable.

Four years prior to this night, at the age of 18, I had attempted to smoke a cigarette. The room began to spin as if it were mounted on some big wheel, and I was sick before the fag had burned down. This, as unbelievable as it may sound, had been my only experience with drugs before Richard's India proposal.

Nevertheless, I listened as Richard explained to me that he could get hash for $50 a pound. This meant very little to me as I had no idea of the street value of hashish, but I told him I'd think about it and get back to him soon.

Later that week, I was at a nightclub in the city and ran into a few friends I had known at De La Salle College in Ashfield, where I went to school. We talked for a while, particularly about how I had been nearly expelled for running a betting scam from class. I'd draw up a form guide in my desk, collect bets from interested classmates and run to the TAB at lunchtime. It worked very well for a while – even some of the teachers were having the odd bet – but it was eventually exposed. One day at assembly, in front of every boy in the school, the headmaster declared that a betting scam had been brought to his attention and the boy responsible should step forward. He said that he knew who the boy was and was giving him one last chance to salvage some dignity and own up. Prior to the assembly, I had been tipped off by various students who believed I had been named to the school staff as the ringleader. Nevertheless, I gambled that he was bluffing and silently stood my ground. After a few moments, the headmaster announced: 'All right, then . . . Warren Fellows, come forward immediately.'

This would not be the last time in my life that I ignored warning signs and walked into an ambush. No doubt, my old school friends assumed that I had continued along such an outlaw path and, coincidentally enough, asked if I was interested in buying some hash. I told them no, but asked, just out of curiosity, how much a pound of hash would fetch on the market. They suggested $1,800 would be about right.

I was dazzled. The money seemed so good that I can honestly say the consequences didn't occur to me at all. The chances of being caught were outweighed by the potential for profit. I made up my mind on the spot.

A few days later I saw Richard and told him I was interested. He explained to me that before we did anything we would have to come up with money for our airfares and accommodation, as well as the deal itself. I told him I'd approach another bookmaker I knew who might stretch me a loan. When I asked the bookmaker for the money, I decided to be straight with him and tell him exactly what it was for. To my astonishment, he agreed right away to the loan, adding: 'I trust you, Warren.'

* * *

I can still feel India. Maybe no one forgets their first trip overseas, and their first impressions of a new land. If I close my eyes, I can smell that hot stench of poverty. I can hear it: the beggars, the filthy, broken people darting about, whole families living and growing in the streets, people so deformed they looked like their bodies had been melted. I remember seeing one woman who was missing most of the features on her face, with festering craters where the features had been, as if they'd fallen off only a few minutes before. And I can vividly recall my most frequent thought during that first day in Madras: 'Why am I here, making this trip? Why do I need the money? I'm not doing so badly.'

We soon met Richard's contact, a man called Rashik, who invited us to stay in his house with his wife and family. He was very accommodating, but, as a drug contact, Rashik proved to be less than sensational after all. When Richard finally mentioned the purpose of our visit, Rashik was horrified. He flatly refused to have anything to do with hashish at this time. Gandhi had declared a national emergency – not an unusual occurrence in India – and the slightest offence carried an immediate two-year jail term. Rashik, a well-connected local, was nervous.

For the next few days there was little else for Richard and me to do but move about, pretend to be tourists and keep our ears open. We soon found ourselves drifting south to Bangalore, the nearest city with a racetrack. Here, we met Ronny Monroe, a Corsican hustler in his mid-forties. For reasons I was never to ascertain, he was banned from entering just about every country in the civilised world, and so had made India his home. While not forthcoming with any advice regarding where to obtain hashish, Ronny seemed the sort of person who might put Richard and me in contact with the right people. He invited us to dinner that night, at the Hotel Bangalore International.

Immediately upon leaving the racetrack, Richard and I were stopped by three policemen. They wanted us to tell them our names and the hotel at which we were staying. Foolishly, Richard told them everything.

That night, at around 6 p.m., there was a knock at the door. I opened it to find the same three policemen who, strangely, walked straight past me and demanded identification from Richard. They then proceeded to search through every piece of luggage Richard owned, while never touching a single thing of mine. As they left, one of them – a captain, I think smiled at me and said, 'Goodnight'. I distinctly remember a peculiar feeling I had at that moment – a feeling that I was in the middle of something I didn't fully understand, and therefore could not be harmed by it. My innocence, I thought, would keep me safe, even when I was guilty.

At dinner that night, Ronny introduced us to many local people. He seemed very well connected.

Midway through the evening, I noticed an Indian man, possibly in his late thirties, slumped on a table in the distance, his head down and his arms outstretched, as if saying a hopeless prayer. Ronny told me his name was Ahma, the owner of the hotel, and soon called him over to our party. Ahma did his best to join our conversation, but seemed very distracted.

All of a sudden, and apparently out of nowhere, the man began to sob. Ronny explained to me that Ahma was heartbroken over a girl who had recently left him. I approached Ahma and tried to offer him the usual sympathy, but he seemed inconsolable. Eventually, I asked him if there was anything I could do to help. He stopped crying, lifted his head and asked me to follow him to the office, where he produced a photo of the girl. Instantly, I understood why Ahma was so devastated.

Her name was Avril. She was astonishingly beautiful, a young French–Indian girl with long black hair and striking blue eyes.

Ahma begged me to go to Avril's home in nearby Cochin and bring her back to him. He said he would pay both myself and Richard $1,000 each, as well as taking care of our airline tickets and accommodation. We would be correcting a terrible wrong, he said, and he would be eternally grateful. The only condition was that at no time was Ahma's name to be mentioned. If we were to drop any names at all, we could only mention Arthur, a jockey in Bangalore with whom Avril was acquainted. Ahma's involvement was to be kept secret from Avril, and we were not to reveal this discussion to anyone else.

I conferred with Richard and we both agreed that it sounded like an interesting diversion. When we accepted Ahma's offer, he again began to sob, only harder than before.

* * *

Three days later, Richard and I arrived in Cochin, and spent the morning lazing about in the lush hotel grounds while trying to form some sort of plan. By mid-afternoon we still hadn't dreamed up anything spectacular, so we decided to go to the address we had been given and just see what unfolded.

Avril's home was surrounded by a high fence, as if containing something that was not to be seen by ordinary people. I noticed that curiosity had grabbed the better of somebody, for a neat spy-hole had been carved into the woodwork. I peered inside, and gazed upon the reason for both the fence and the spy-hole.

Avril was sitting on the back steps, wearing nothing but a pair of white shorts. She was gently combing her hair, which cascaded like a deep, black waterfall down the entire length of her back. Never before or since have I seen anything so gorgeously exotic. Ahma's grief was making even more sense to me now, for I was beginning to feel heartbroken myself.

We returned to the front of the house and knocked on the door. Avril's mother answered, and we explained that we were friends of Arthur's, who had told us to come and visit Avril while we were holidaying in Cochin. She smiled and invited us in for tea and biscuits.

Avril seemed cautious at first, but, as we spoke, I could see both her and her mother relaxing in our company. I couldn't take my eyes off Avril, and was working to the point of exhaustion to disguise my every intention. After a time, I nervously asked whether they would both like to accompany Richard and I to dinner that evening. To my surprise, they accepted the offer immediately.

We took them to the finest restaurant we could find and ordered several bottles of champagne. Over the course of the evening, I would sometimes catch Avril's eye and my heart would thump. I knew then that I was falling for her completely. I was too hypnotised by my own feelings to dare remember that we were drinking Ahma's champagne.

Later in the night, Avril asked me if I would like to join her for a walk in the gardens. I was so overwhelmed I could scarcely rise from the table. As we walked through the grounds, Avril talked of her dreams of finding a better place for herself and her mother, her desire to escape, her gnawing feelings of confinement. She asked me plenty about myself and what I was doing in Cochin, and I very nearly crumbled under the weight of my own lies. She stopped by a flowerbed, picked one with large white petals, turned and handed it to me. Then we kissed. I was utterly lost to this girl.

Later, back at our hotel, I talked with Richard about what had occurred. He suggested that if anything romantic happened between Avril and me it could be disastrous for both of us – as emotionally broken as he was, Ahma did not seem an unpowerful man. We decided that the safest thing we could do was to return to Bangalore and claim that Avril had refused to come with us.

* * *

A few moments after entering the foyer of the Hotel Bangalore International, we saw Ahma dashing towards us, a look of desperation in his eyes. Had we succeeded? Where was Avril? As we explained that she had not wanted to return with us, his face sagged with disappointment. He continued to probe for answers, as if not accepting our explanations. Eventually, he requested that I see him alone in his office. Once there, Ahma turned, looked me directly in the eye and declared: 'I know that you can bring her back. I know that if anyone can bring her back to me, it is you. I need you to return to Cochin.'

There was something new in Ahma's voice now. He was no longer weakened and insipid, but forceful and determined. I knew there was no way he could have known about what had happened between Avril and me, but something told me he did. What's more, it seemed that he didn't care – so long as it brought Avril home to him.

I don't know if I relented because I felt for him or because of my own feelings for Avril. To this day I don't know.

Whatever the case, I returned to Cochin two days later. When I arrived at Avril's house, she ran to the front gate to meet me. She was overjoyed that I had returned and smothered me in affection. For the next few days we were never out of each other's sight. It was bliss.

One evening, Avril took me out on a motorbike to an old village. It was as if we had been transported back to some primitive age: mud huts for houses, no vehicles or machinery whatsoever, women sitting in their huts grinding grain for bread. In the centre of the village, some bizarre ritual was taking place. I could see a woman writhing in the dirt, throwing up what looked like parts of her internal organs. There was a man dressed in white and draped in many beads, standing over her and chanting things I could not understand. Avril explained to me that voodoo was still practised in Cochin, that this woman was possessed and was about to undergo an exorcism performed by a white witch. At that moment, a woman appeared carrying a live chicken. The man in white chanted some more, then the woman cut off the chicken's head, causing the headless body to dash crazily about. When it finally came to rest in the dirt, the woman on the ground seemed to relax, as if what had possessed her now possessed the dying body of the chicken.

As I had never seen anything like this before, it naturally disturbed me. Avril, on the other hand, seemed perfectly at ease with it all, as if she was in touch with some other-worldliness that I couldn't possibly fathom.

* * *

One night, Avril and I were in my hotel room when the phone rang. It was Ahma. My heart pounded so hard I was sure he could hear it in Bangalore. I had to be shrewd, convincing Ahma I was alone while, at the same time, disguising the caller's identity from Avril.

'Have you seen her?'

'Yes.'

'Is she returning with you?'

'I don't know yet.'

Avril began to look curious and a little concerned. I smiled at her as I said to Ahma: 'I'll call you back when I know.'

As soon as the call was concluded, Avril asked who the caller had been. I told her it was Richard, inquiring as to when I would be returning to Bangalore.

Hearing Ahma's voice had suddenly reminded me of my real purpose for being in Cochin. In that moment, I might have broken down and told Avril everything, but a strange sense of duty forced me to continue with my deception instead.

I asked Avril if she would consider coming to Bangalore with me, as I could not bear to leave her behind. At first, she said no – she didn't like Bangalore and, as much as she wanted to be with me, she had no desire to return to that place. I pressed her for an explanation but she simply shook her head. I pleaded with her, promising that I would not leave her side and would return her to Cochin at any time she wished. Finally, she agreed to come with me, but on the condition that we travelled by car. She did not wish to be seen at the airport. This aroused my curiosity, but I decided not to press her further for fear that she may change her mind.

I called Ahma and explained the situation to him. Not surprisingly, he was thrilled. He told me to hire a taxi for the trip – he would pay the driver when we arrived in Bangalore.

The mixed feelings that swam in my head during that journey almost defy description. I was overcome by love for Avril, but driven by a sense of obligation to Ahma. In succeeding for him, I was betraying her. I had no idea what would happen when we arrived, but Avril's apprehension was beginning to unsettle me. I was caught in the middle of a situation which had no comfortable resolution that I could imagine. By the time we reached the outskirts of

Bangalore, I was convinced I had made a dreadful mistake.

As our taxi pulled to a halt outside the Hotel Bangalore International, Avril stiffened and paled with fear. When I asked her what was wrong, she simply shook her head and refused to get out of the vehicle. But it was too late, for Ahma had seen the taxi and was already racing towards us. He was obviously delighted to see Avril. The look on her face, however, was a fusion of terror and defeat. She turned to me as if begging an explanation for why I had betrayed her. I felt sick.

Ahma whisked Avril out of the cab and into the hotel before I could so much as take a breath. I went to my room to think about what had happened and what I was going to do now.

* * *

The following evening, I went to the bar and inquired after Avril. Nobody seemed to know of her whereabouts, and there was something conspiratorial about the way they all denied knowledge of her existence. Eventually, I spotted Ronny Monroe and told him what had happened. He glared at me with genuine astonishment as I revealed everything – our mission at Ahma's request, the journey to Cochin, me and Avril. To my horror, Ronny explained how Avril was virtually a prisoner here, that Ahma even had an apartment specially built for her where she remained under armed guard. Each evening, Ahma would escort Avril to the hotel restaurant, where she would play guitar to entertain the guests, then return her to her room at the evening's end. She had escaped once before and, now that I had brought her back, it was doubtful that Ahma would let her out of his sight again.

I asked Ronny to tell me where the apartment was. He knew instantly what I was thinking and told me I was a fool, that Ahma was not a man to mess with, but I insisted. Quite apart from my feelings for Avril, I knew I would never live with myself if I left without trying to reverse the predicament I had helped engineer for this person. Eventually, Ronny told me that the apartment was on the third floor of the hotel, with two sentries armed with .303 rifles guarding the entrance to the stairway on the ground floor.

Before nightfall, I conducted a basic reconnaissance of the building and found what looked to be a way to the balcony adjoining Avril's apartment. It was a bit of a heroic long shot but I was determined to give it a try.

The following day, when I heard that Ahma was absent from the hotel, I climbed out of a window on the fourth floor, crept down the sloping roof and swung onto the landing below. I waited outside Avril's door for a few moments and, when I was sure there was nobody else in the apartment with her, I knocked. Avril answered, pulled me inside and quickly closed the door. Though pleased to see me, she was terrified. She said that if Ahma discovered us together we would both be doomed. As briefly as I could, I explained to her why things had worked out the way they did, how I had betrayed her unwittingly and would do everything I could to help her escape. It was an anxious few minutes. It was also one of the most loving moments of my life. By the time I left Avril's little prison, we had agreed to be married.

Over the next few days, I desperately tried to find a priest who would marry us so that I could bring Avril back to Australia. But everywhere I went, I was told that I had to wait three months before we could go through the correct legal process in court.

Time was running out for me and Avril. While I'd been concerning myself with her, Ronny had uncovered a contact through whom he could obtain some excellent quality Kashmiri hashish, and Richard had organised somebody who could construct suitcases with false interiors. We would be leaving India in a few days.

Two nights before we left, I returned to see Avril one more time. I explained to her the problem with getting married and told her that, although I had to go, I would come back for her soon. It was an emotional and passionate farewell. Avril asked that I leave her something of mine, something for her to remember me by until I returned. I gave her the only item I had in my pockets – a comb. I told her it was an appropriate gift, as the first time I had seen her she had been combing her hair. We cried together as we embraced, promising each other we'd wait.

* * *

During the following day, before leaving India, I was strolling down the street when I came across the dwelling of a fortune-teller. I stepped inside and was greeted by a woman so old and frail it seemed she would have enough trouble seeing the present, let alone the future. Nevertheless, I sat opposite her in the darkness, and her opening utterances filled me with a mixture of fascination and dread.

She told me exactly when I was born, to the very time of day, and I had told her nothing. She then went on to tell me that when I turned 25 years old I would enter into ten years of very bad luck, whereupon I would suffer untold loss. In this time, I would be afflicted with a terrible sickness, but it would not kill me. She then revealed that there was a woman in my life of whom I should beware. This woman, she said, was evil, and I was not to let her get any article of my clothing or a single strand of my hair. As I rose to leave, she told me I would never again return to India, and warned that I should be careful at airports.

* * *

Returning from that first trip to India was almost a catastrophe.

We caught a domestic flight to Madras where we would connect with our flight home to Australia. As we approached the customs bay, with our bags pre-packed with hashish, we noticed something that shook us to the core: customs officials were checking every single suitcase or bag that went through the luggage area. They were being very thorough, with every item being ruthlessly scrutinised then marked with a chalk 'X' when it had passed inspection. The hash in our suitcases was sufficiently concealed to pass a routine inspection, but there was no way its discovery would go unnoticed here. Richard and I had to think fast. We agreed to pretend that we had lost the keys to the suitcases and engage in a wild argument which, hopefully, would create some kind of diversion.

When the official asked me to open the bags, I turned to Richard and asked for the keys. He replied that he didn't have them, that I had never given the keys to him at all. So began the mock brawl that culminated in me throwing a phony tantrum and kicking the hell out of the suitcases, as if I wanted to break them open. The officials must have assumed that anyone who would want to break open their suitcases must not be concealing anything illegal inside. He tried to calm me down, told me my anger was unnecessary, marked the bags with an 'X' and hurriedly ushered us through.

But we were not out of the soup yet. We had a stopover in Singapore, where we were to change planes and show our inoculation cards and passports. As we reached the authorities, Richard discovered that he had packed his inoculation documents in one of the suitcases. I thought the authorities might let it drift, but they stood firm, saying one of us would have to be escorted down to the luggage area and retrieve the documents from our baggage. Believing myself a better actor than Richard, I volunteered to go. Playing the role of the innocent, jovial angel was an excruciating task as I searched through the suitcases with an armed guard looking over my shoulder. Eventually, I found the relevant papers and we got through Singapore.

While standing at the terminal in Sydney, waiting for our bags to appear on the revolving carousel, it became apparent that I had dealt the suitcases a more brutal thrashing in Madras than they could handle. One of them had split at the seams, and it looked as though the slightest touch would cause it to come completely apart, spilling bags of hashish onto the concourse. For a moment I considered cutting our losses and leaving them on the carousel, but I then realised the authorities would have no difficulty tracing them to Richard and myself. I quickly snatched the bags from the conveyor belt, threw them onto a trolley and made my way through the gates, boldly announcing I had nothing to declare. I was through.

Once again, good fortune seemed to have shielded me from every potentially disastrous onslaught.

* * *

I was to see Avril once more. Several months later, I was in India on another job. Passing by the Hotel Bangalore International, I caught a glimpse of her, quite a distance away, sitting in the front gardens, her head bowed toward the ground. I was compelled to stop and stare at her for a moment. As if sensing I was there, Avril slowly raised her head and met my gaze. She was still as enchanting as ever, but there was an expression on her face which I had never seen before. It was nothing – no surprise, no love, no hostility, nothing – as if she were staring into total darkness.

Then she simply bowed her head toward the ground and continued combing her hair, which cascaded like a deep, black waterfall down the entire length of her back.

I tell this story to show just how reckless I was at this time in my life. The fact is, by the time I returned to India I had found another. She was with me on this occasion when I saw Avril. I was so shortsighted, so easily impressed and distracted that I couldn't even maintain my own feelings, no matter how deep or intense, for any decent stretch of time.

I was the perfect person to become a drug courier.

* * *

What followed this tour of India is basically a story of greed. Mine.

But, wherever there is room for greed, there will always be a cast of thousands: people who are crooked.

Some have since grown up to become decent members of society, while others, like myself, simply had the crookedness bludgeoned out of us. I don't wish to expose such people unnecessarily – there can be no future in that for anybody. This is the major reason why many names in this story are changed or deleted entirely.

There are, of course, some people in this story who, to this day, are still crooked. I hear tales of them from time to time, like rumoured sightings of Elvis. For me to name such people outright would be to ensure that I was murdered before you opened your next Christmas present. I won't be doing it.

In any case, this is the story of what I did, and what became of me because of it. It is not my business to prosecute anyone else, and it's not my wish to do so either. They can do that themselves. Or leave it to God, or the laws of nature, or mathematics – it doesn't matter. There are a few notable exceptions, but I'll tell you about them later.

One of the changes that occurred when I returned to Sydney was that I got married and fathered a child. And that is as much as I wish to say about my wife and son. They have little bearing on this story and I'd much rather leave them be. Today, they have rebuilt their lives and I have no desire to revive the agony they suffered, for the sake of a few colourful mentions in a book. It breaks my heart to think of them. When you incarcerate someone, guilty or not, you incarcerate the innocents who love them, and there are always such people. The most vile murderer of all time had a mother.

For entirely different reasons, there is another person I would like to leave out of this story. I'd like to forget he ever existed. But I cannot forget and cannot leave him out – he is a pivotal player in my life and one of the reasons why I am who I am today, and not who I once was.

His name is William Sinclair. To even mention those two words makes me uneasy, as if the mere utterance will somehow come to life in some ghostly form of the human being. I wish I could tell you why I feel this way about him, but I dare not. I don't want to utter his name again in this story. I will refer to him from now on as 'The Old Man'.

I became aware of The Old Man in the bar in Wynyard, where this whole affair began. He used to do a fair amount of punting there, particularly with a guy known as 'The Bookmaker'. The Old Man called himself a businessman, but never really elaborated on what, exactly, his business was. Sometimes, it was 'travel consultant', other times it was 'finance broker'. It appeared that he was very wealthy. He would wander about introducing himself with this slinky façade of nobility, complete with a phony regal accent. The truth is that he was, in fact, innocent of the particular crime for which he was later incarcerated, but he was certainly no babe in the woods. He was cunning and ruthless and cared about nobody but himself. There was no way I could have known this at first, but I was to learn.

The Old Man had heard of my courier exploits – probably from Richard, with whom I had fallen out over an unrelated matter – and began sniffing around. It became obvious to me that he wanted to be part of the action. In order to do so, however, he would have to get rid of The Bookmaker, and he was soon to get his chance.

Over the next few months I began to travel extensively on The Bookmaker's ticket. I made trips to Hawaii, Los Angeles and various regions in South America to obtain cocaine. During one of these journeys, a contact fled with some of The Bookmaker's money and never returned with the goods. Everybody knows this is a common occurrence in the drug world, so it was with a fair amount of embarrassment and concern that I phoned The Bookmaker to let him know. To my relief, he accepted my story and told me we'd sort it out when I returned.

In my absence, however, The Old Man had heard of my trouble and seized the opportunity to sully my relationship with The Bookmaker, telling him that I had pocketed the money myself and could not be trusted. The ploy was successful enough, for after my return The Bookmaker began harassing me for the money he now claimed I owed him.

One night at the Wynyard bar, two men who I had never seen before approached me and began to slap me around. They said that I owed somebody money and should pay it or there would be serious trouble. The blows became more and more ferocious until I assured them I'd solve the problem before the end of the week. The following day I approached The Bookmaker who, I immediately assumed, was feigning shock and confusion at my battered appearance. I told him I intended to pay him the money he wanted, but simply did not have such an amount at that time. He was silent for a moment, then dropped the apparent façade, saying he was sorry this had happened to me but, yes, I did owe him money and he would appreciate its return. I do, however, recall that The Bookmaker did seem genuinely sorry and still bewildered by the whole thing.

Later, as I was racking my brain for ways to raise the money, The Old Man appeared and, like some sort of walking coincidence, announced that he could help.

CHAPTER 2

THAILAND

THAILAND HAS NEVER been successfully invaded. That always struck me as surprising, considering the country's attractive geographical position. But maybe it's because the Thais, like the Vietnamese, are an incredibly durable race of people and their patience would win them a war of attrition. Also, when their patience expires, they are perhaps the cruellest people in the world. That's not an enemy anyone wants to fight.

And Thailand will probably stay uninvaded for a while. The country is such a shambles in every way, only a nation of complete idiots would want to inherit it. Or a nation of heroin addicts.

Heroin is so easy to get in Thailand it's a joke. On my first trip to Bangkok, the cab driver who I hailed at the airport asked me two questions: where I wanted to go and whether I wanted any drugs. The people in the villages have been cultivating and smoking opium for thousands of years and don't understand what the international fuss is about. Westerners tell them they're doing something illegal and these poor people are seriously confused. For them, it's as traditional as drinking alcohol is for us.

So it is probably because of international pressure alone that the government of Thailand imposes brutal consequences on those who try to export drugs. If heroin was legalised worldwide, Thailand would stand to become the financial superpower of the Asia Pacific.

Nevertheless, while tolerating the situation in the countryside, the Thai government likes to come down hard on trafficking. It's all a bit absurd, when you think about it. It's like going to a supermarket to buy coffee, finding masses of it on the shelves, taking some to the checkout and getting arrested.

There is a disturbing aspect to how the government encourages the police to get the job done. Thailand offers its police a financial incentive for drug-related arrests. I'm not actually sure if this is still the case today, but it was certainly the case in 1978 – I got it from the horse's mouth. What's interesting is that this incentive was not a flat fee, but a percentage of the street value of the drugs seized in the arrest. Considering that Thai police are not very high wage-earners, this has to be an unsettling situation for the innocent traveller.

While the point I'm trying to make here should be obvious, I will declare, once and for all, that I was not one of these innocent travellers. But I have heard some frightening stories. Of course, if all the jails in the world were emptied of those who claimed to have been framed, there'd be nobody left inside but some very bored guards. But, even if you don't know them like I do, it's surely ridiculous to believe that the police force of a country as messed-up as Thailand don't indulge in moments of greed and corruption. And all you have to do is have the bad luck to be there when that moment happens. I wouldn't travel to Thailand again for anything in this life.

* * *

I don't know how many times I went to Bangkok. I wasn't counting. There are only two that matter. The first is when I went to meet The Old Man. He'd become enamoured with some Thai woman and wanted to get married and live in Bangkok. I met him in a hotel on Patpong Road called The Texan Bar, which he was trying to buy. With him was an Australian man who was helping him with finance. His name was Neddy Smith.

I've got to say that I liked Neddy instantly. He seemed a very genuine person who would do anything for you. The fact that he would go on to become one of Australia's most notorious criminals was just not apparent. Several times during the evening, The Old Man pulled me aside and warned me not to get too friendly with Neddy. He said he was a bad man and one who must be kept at a careful distance. Coming from The Old Man, this was a pretty admirable reference, so Ned and I proceeded to hit it off. By the end of the evening, it was obvious Ned and I would be keeping in touch when we returned to Australia.

Also on this trip, I met a man who told me he could get a large amount of excellent quality heroin very cheaply, and that he knew people in Australia who I could sell it to at a vast profit. I baulked for a moment about heroin – as far as drugs go, it's the final stop and I knew that – but I decided fairly quickly that I'd go ahead and take that last step. It was purely a financial decision.

No doubt the people who write letters to newspapers and ring radio stations declaring that all drug pushers must die would think I'm nothing but an animal for making such an apparently quick and easy choice here. But I can't think like that, even now. So President Harry Truman agonised for three weeks over whether to drop the Atom Bomb on Japan. He still did it, didn't he? Even after giving himself time to think about the innocent women and children he'd incinerate. The families of those people would surely view Truman's three weeks of thinking time as a bit of an insult. No, it's better if the truth be told: I did it without thinking of anything but the money. It was swift and greedy and ignorant. But, for me, it was not murder. I didn't see my victims. I didn't think of them. I didn't even know for sure if there would be any victims at all. I was careless and thoughtless, but, in my mind at the time I was no more a murderer than the man at the pub who sells beer to alcoholics.

* * *

On my way back to Australia there was trouble on the plane: there were four men getting very boisterously drunk, sitting right behind me. Out of the corner of my eye, I noticed they were wearing suits. I tried to forget about them for a while, but my instincts were soon proved correct as their conversation turned to work. They were detectives.

Sometime after this realisation, the captain's voice came over the intercom, informing us that there was a problem at Sydney airport and the plane was to be diverted for a landing at Melbourne instead. I became deeply concerned. How did they know? Were the detectives pretending to be drunk, just to put me at ease?

By the time the plane landed, I was feeling a little more comfortable about the detectives. They were plastered. I was sure that they couldn't have been involved in any surveillance of me, as they were having enough trouble seeing their way out of the plane. I decided to stay close behind them. I, too, was wearing a suit and thought it might be good luck to be seen as part of their happy little party. As we waited for our luggage to appear on the carousel, I turned and made a joke to one of the detectives, who laughed and answered very casually. Everything seemed to be fine now. But as I turned from the carousel, suitcase in hand, I noticed something that put a rock in my stomach – every passenger from our flight was being searched by a bumper troupe of customs officers. I was convinced this was the end for me, but remained close to the detectives who, I thought, through some stroke of luck, might be my only chance.

As we approached the customs bays, I turned to the same detective I'd joked with before and made some other gag, making sure that one of the officers would see it. Once again, the detective howled laughing and spluttered back some sort of retort. At that moment, the detective at the front of our group began to speak to one of the officers. He might also have shown his badge – I'm not sure. He then turned and somewhat drunkenly gestured towards the other detectives, as if to point out who was in his group. The officer waved them through and they began to move. I moved with them. The officer stared at me for a moment and I began to feel I was moving in slow motion. What if the forward detective had made it perfectly clear who was in his party? What if one of the others turned around to declare I was not with them? Against every urge in my body, I stared straight back at the officer and, doing my best to look as drunk as my 'chums', smiled and nodded politely. To my relief, he smiled back and ushered me through. The detectives were too drunk to even bother looking back at the heroin trafficker they had escorted through customs.

I immediately got to a phone and called my contact in Sydney. He had been having a heart attack ever since hearing that the plane had been diverted to Melbourne and couldn't believe that I'd made it through safely.

'You're a genius, Warren,' he kept repeating. 'A bloody genius.'

* * *

A few weeks later, Neddy called me and we went for a drink at a pub in Kingsford. Apparently, word had spread about my little Melbourne experience. Neddy was impressed with my calm under fire and, over the course of the afternoon, expressed an interest in me coming to work for him. He had plenty to do for a man who could stay cool when everyone around was losing their heads. I remember very clearly him saying to me: 'Warren, I could go and beat the life out of someone twice my size, then sit down somewhere and eat my lunch. Not a problem. But there's no way I could ever walk through customs with a suitcase full of drugs. I capitulate on that score.'

Sometime later, Ned took me for a ride in his car, allegedly to go to another pub. Halfway there, however, he pulled up outside a house, telling me to wait as he was just ducking in to see a friend. A few minutes later he emerged and, as he climbed into the driver's seat, I noticed he had some sort of bundle under his jacket.

Suddenly, he whipped out a handgun, held it to my head and, with a murderous smirk I'll never forget, said: 'Sorry, Sunshine, this is it.'

I was so petrified I don't think any expression registered on my face at all. A million thoughts dashed through my head. Had I slighted Ned in some way? Unwittingly encroached on his turf? Had I been set up by The Old Man?

Suddenly, Ned broke into that broad, friendly smile and lowered the pistol from my temple. He was joking, he said, and had just wanted to see how I reacted.

But even then I knew that this was no joke at all. The entire purpose of that terrifying few seconds was to gauge whether I really was as cool under fire as he had been led to believe.

Ned flipped the pistol over and handed it to me butt first, asking me to put it in the glovebox for him. Sensing this might be another test, I refused, telling him to put it in the glovebox himself. He insisted for a short time, but finally smiled again and threw the piece in the glovebox himself. We continued on to another pub for yet another round of beers.

Ned was insistent I come to work for him now. I told him about The Old Man and he said not to worry, that The Old Man looked as if he were going to stay in Bangkok and wouldn't be able to provide me with work for much longer. Ned said he didn't need me to do much – just carry money here and there, run the odd errand, that sort of thing. Eventually I agreed.

Ned then rose from the table and asked me if I wanted to come with him now, as he was going to see a man about something. I thought about that gun in the glovebox of his car and declared that I'd rather stay and have a few more beers. The usual few moments of insistence followed, ending with Ned saying he'd call me tomorrow and leaving the hotel to run his errand alone.

I often think about that afternoon. Did Ned ever find the man he was looking for? What happened if he did? And what would've become of me if I had taken that gun from his hand, placing my prints all over the butt? Would Ned have done that to me? Would I have been saddled with murder? And in light of everything that has happened, I often wonder if that would have been so bad.

* * *

Over the next few months I got to know Neddy well. We went out together a few times and I became pretty fond of him as a mate. I never saw the flashpoint streak of violence that he has since been credited with – most of the time, Ned was just being an average bloke. He was a good-looking guy, so he never had any problems speaking to either men or women.

Despite this, I had become increasingly aware of the fact that Neddy was on the outside of the law, and a very well-placed outsider at that. I noted that police would contact him from time to time, pre-warning him of raids that were about to be conducted on the homes of his friends. Although I was participating in illegal deals at this time, I was a little alarmed as I saw the web spreading. Police, other criminals, rich businessmen – everyone seemed to know Neddy Smith. And everyone was frightened of him. Everyone.

I'm sure you're wondering how I could've wished to involve myself with someone like this, and today I often wonder that myself. The only explanation I can give for my actions is that I was young and impressionable. Ned made me feel impressed with myself. To me at that age, being liked by a man most people were terrified of was flattering.

I was around at his house on the day of his daughter's birthday. Neddy doted on Jamie and he loved his family. On this day there was a knock at the door. Ned answered it to see two policemen standing there, telling him they wished to take him down to the station for questioning. At first, Ned was more or less amused.

'It's my daughter's birthday, for Christ's sake,' he half-laughed. 'Can't it wait till tomorrow?'

The policemen, both a little green and full of young cop gung ho, demanded that Ned come with them immediately. Or else.

Ned's mood changed in a flash. With absolutely every ounce of humanity gone from his voice, he told them, in more of a hiss than a normal voice, that if they were to take him away from his little girl and his family he would find them later and kill them. One of the policemen, boldly but with a hint of fear, began to urge Ned not to say anything stupid. Ned, more authoritatively now, replied that he was being neither stupid nor flippant – they had come to his door and they now had the choice to either leave without him or die, pure and simple. I was stunned. I had never heard Ned say anything like that to anyone, let alone a couple of policemen. As it turned out, they were more stunned than I was. And where I was unsure as to whether Ned meant what he was saying, they most certainly were not. Within seconds they had left, delivering an insipid set of demands as they retreated down the drive.

Neddy Smith, above everything else, was a murderously devoted family man. He wanted the best for himself and his family. Anyone who stood in the way of that dream was in serious trouble.

* * *

The Old Man was becoming a thorn in Neddy's side. Rumour had it that he was drinking a bottle of brandy a day in the Texan Bar. By late afternoon, he was shattered. He'd ring Neddy at ridiculous times of the night and begin talking all sorts of nonsense on the phone. Ned was, perhaps quite rationally, nervous about any conversations regarding business that took place on his home phone. He'd tell The Old Man to knock it off then hang up on him. The following evening, The Old Man would ring again, as staggering drunk as the night before. Ned was losing his patience. He'd invested a lot of money in The Old Man's loony enterprises and was getting nothing from it all but irritation.

One night, Ned met with me in a pub and was furious. He'd just returned from Bangkok where he had met with The Old Man to discuss this business. Drunk in the Texan Bar, The Old Man had introduced him to a complete stranger and then proceeded to talk quite openly about whether Ned was at all interested in the heroin trade. Apparently, Ned went berserk, telling The Old Man to wake up to himself and not talk about such stuff, particularly in the company of strangers. Despite The Old Man's insistence that his new friend could be trusted, Ned closed the conversation and left. Upon return to Australia, Ned did his homework and discovered that the man in question had been a member of the Welsh SAS and had probably been placed in Thailand as an operative for the Commonwealth police. God only knows what sort of grave The Old Man was digging for himself, but Ned wanted no part of it. The Old Man had to go.

Sometime after this I met the man who would become my best friend for the next 13 years. His name was Paul Hayward.

Paul was a champion sportsman and a better man than anyone I've known. As a boxer, he had been chosen to represent Australia in the Montreal Olympic Games in 1976, but shortly afterwards signed a book deal with a publishing company, making him professional and so disqualifying him from amateur sporting contests. That's the kind of person he was – he'd do what he wanted in his heart to do, and not what he thought would impress others most. He was strong in heart and body and spirit. I remember one time, very early on in our acquaintanceship, somebody in a bar was harassing me in some mindless way. I didn't care much – whatever they were attacking me about was trifling to me – but Paul took offence on my behalf, telling the offender, in a forceful but compassionate manner, to move away and just let everyone enjoy the night. We were virtually strangers, yet here he was sticking his neck out for me. Of course, he was a boxer and didn't have too much to fear from some lout in a pub, but he needn't have bothered either. If you were in his circle in the slightest way, he considered it his duty as a strong man to defend you. I thought that was pretty special.

Paul's career as a professional footballer with the Newtown Rugby League club was in top flight when I met him in 1978. There was absolutely no reason for him to be involved in the events that followed. All he did to achieve his place in this sorry tale is marry Gail, the sister of Neddy Smith's de facto wife. And that is how he met Warren Fellows.

Paul had done the odd favour for Neddy, but he had never dealt in the international drug scene. And, really, he never did. Paul's job in Bangkok was to take some money to a friend of Neddy's. Neddy knew that I was going to Bangkok and suggested to Paul that he might like to go along with me.

I'm not sure if Paul already knew about my drug-carrying career up to that point, but he certainly knew what I was going to Bangkok for this time. As I have said, I liked Paul and couldn't possibly have made him an unwitting accomplice. So I told him exactly what I was doing. He was a little apprehensive at first, but eventually agreed to come.

I myself was apprehensive about this particular trip. On my last visit to Bangkok, I had found myself in a compromising position which forced me to abandon a large quantity of drugs in a place where they could easily have been found by the authorities. Had the Thai police been determined enough, I thought, they may have linked me to the drugs by now.

In order to disguise my entry into Thailand, I decided to obtain a false passport, so I approached a friend who I knew could arrange such things. Not long afterwards, I was furnished with my new identity: Gregory Hastings Barker, born on 25 March 1952. My friend had obtained this by going to a cemetery and wandering around until he came across the grave of someone born around the same time as myself. The gravestone told of how Gregory Barker had died unexpectedly at the age of 14 months, before he had a chance to make a mark on society records. I would now step into his place.

I feel the need to apologise to the parents of Gregory Hastings Barker for dragging the memory of their child into this business. But, if they are still alive today, I'm sure they would rather I not speak to them at all.

CHAPTER 3

SIGNS

ABOUT A WEEK before we were due to leave for Thailand, I was at the races and a friend approached me with some alarming news. A policeman from Manly had called his stepfather and asked him what his son's business was with Warren Fellows. The man replied that we were just old friends.

'Well,' said the policeman, 'tell your son to keep away from him, because we've got Fellows under surveillance . . . we think he's involved with a pretty large drug courier operation.'

There are few warnings that could have been more definitive: a policeman saying he and his workmates were watching my every move.

The next day, Paul and I went to see Neddy and told him about the Manly policeman. I expected Ned to be staggered by the news, but, incredibly, he couldn't have cared less. He seemed almost amused. This whole affair was becoming far too strange for me, and I immediately declared my intention to pull out of the deal.

But Neddy wouldn't have it. He insisted that if the police were truly in touch with anything me and Paul were up to, he would have heard so by now. This seemed to make some sense at the time. As I have said, while not fully comprehending the depth of Neddy's involvement with the police, I knew that he was well informed of their movements. Nevertheless, I was spooked, and so was Paul. He was fairly apprehensive and our combined panic was feeding on itself. Sensing this, Neddy started to get a little firm. He had been counting on Paul to take some money to The Old Man for him. Paul wouldn't go if I didn't, and I didn't want to go at all. Ned lost his patience. He didn't exactly threaten us, but rather intimated that we were letting him down. He was well aware of what we'd be thinking; that we may be placing ourselves at greater risk by letting down Neddy than by going to Bangkok. We were backed into a corner.

When you're in a situation like this, it is extremely difficult to get out. In any secret society, leaving the fold is frowned upon – you are going out into the world with the secrets of the brotherhood. You become a risk. And, in many ways, it seems safer to remain inside. When I think of it, I think of a cube. If you're on the outside of a cube, the angles and edges seem harsh, the corners sharp. If you come too close, or try to get in, you can be hurt. But when you're on the inside of the cube, the boundaries are softer, just flat walls and corners that you can safely nestle into. From the inside, it feels more like a circle. If it rolls over, those on the outside will be damaged, not you.

And so, reluctantly, we agreed to go. I booked the airline tickets and the hotel rooms for our arrival on Tuesday, three days away. Neddy has since claimed that Paul and I were undone because I booked the airline tickets from Neddy's home phone. I honestly cannot remember whether I did that or not. It's possible. Whatever the case, I don't think it matters much. The tickets were booked two days before we left. I have since discovered that the police were right behind us by then.

Unbeknownst to me, a certain policeman in Thailand had been waiting for me to return since February.

In the afternoon of 2 October 1978 Paul and I caught a cab to the home of a man who regularly drove for Neddy. He was to drive us to the airport, as we had arranged earlier in the day. When we arrived, however, there was no sign of him and the house was apparently empty. This struck me as definitely odd, but we were running late and had no time to stand around pondering the possibilities. We continued on in the taxi and made it in plenty of time to take our seats on Qantas Flight 5 to Bangkok. Midway over the ocean, Paul turned to me and spoke the first words he'd spoken all afternoon: 'I think we've had it.'

* * *

Outside Don Muang airport in Bangkok, our regular contact, Noi, was waiting for us in his Black Cab. As he drove into town, he seemed agitated. I asked him what was wrong, and he told me that two Chinese men had just been executed for drug offences. He was a little edgy, that's all. He dropped us at the Montien Hotel, where we had two rooms booked for myself and Paul. I told Noi to return in three days' time, whereupon we would organise the heroin deal.

The following day, Paul wanted to go for a drink at the Texan Bar in Patpong Road. I was not comfortable about doing this. Before our departure from Australia, Neddy had warned us to stay clear of The Old Man, who was, from this time onwards, to be excluded from all our affairs. We decided to do some shopping instead, and the first shop we entered was Natty Gems, a jewellery store where I had purchased emeralds on one of my previous visits. As I stepped through the doorway, I nearly collided with The Old Man. He was his usual self – it was splendid to see me, it was splendid to see Paul, the whole aching world was splendid – and he wasted no time in insisting that we join him for a drink. I knew that he would be intensely curious as to the meaning of our appearance in Bangkok, but I saw no point in trying to avoid him any longer and so I accepted. During our conversation, The Old Man battled in vain to extract information from both of us, but we remained tight-lipped. There was no way I was going to divulge anything, and Paul knew that Neddy and I had now firmly made up our minds and The Old Man was out. Over the course of an hour, he became increasingly frustrated and angry.

The irony of this little scene is laughable. For, unbeknownst to us all, we were being watched, and The Old Man's obvious display of desperation was later used as proof of his involvement.

On Thursday, Noi contacted me with the news that he was having some trouble getting the heroin, as he needed the money up front. I told him to come to the hotel, whereupon I gave him the money, assuring him that his own fee would be paid to him when he returned. By Saturday evening, I still hadn't heard from him and began to worry. But I can clearly remember a battle in my head between the feelings of terror and relief. Considering the reticence I had displayed to Neddy prior to my departure, I knew that he would not believe some story about Noi going missing with the cash. He'd sooner believe that Paul and I had lost our nerve and allowed it to happen. Nevertheless, deep down, the thought of travelling home empty-handed was a soothing one. Since this particular journey had begun, I'd felt my luck – the charm that had seen me through years of this business – had been left behind in Manly.

No sooner was I getting comfortable with this scenario when Noi called. He told me not to worry, as everything was okay now.

The following day he arrived at the Montien Hotel and I picked up two bags from the back seat of his cab. I gave him his fee and told him he'd receive another $4,000 when he returned on Wednesday morning to take Paul and I to the airport. Back in my room, I checked the contents of the bags and, when I was satisfied, transferred the heroin into a suitcase I had purchased for the trip home. Paul suggested that it was wise if we kept the suitcase in his room, as he had less reason to be suspected by authorities than I.

Over the next few days, however, Paul became increasingly paranoid. On the night before we were to depart for Australia, we went for a drink together in another bar in Patpong Road. Paul spoke nervously about the heroin, and his apprehension showed in his every movement. To pacify him, I volunteered to take the suitcase from his room for the duration of our stay. It seemed to calm him somewhat.

Late into the evening, we drank and talked for a while about what we would do when we returned to Australia. Paul said this experience had unsettled him, and he declared his intention not to do anything like it again. After a time, we both felt quite tired and decided to return to our rooms to sleep for a while.

As we entered the foyer of the Montien Hotel, the concierge called out and asked me to come to the desk. As I approached, he turned, removed a slip of paper from my letterbox and handed it to me. It was from Noi: 'Sorry. Can't pick you up tomorrow. Busy.'

The warning bells started to clang in my head. The idea of Noi being 'too busy' to make the easiest $4,000 of his life seemed totally absurd. The driver in Sydney, now the driver here – we were being deserted.

I knew this information would send Paul into a state of wild alarm, so I decided to keep it to myself for the time being.

We went to Paul's room and talked for a while. We were quite drunk, so I don't remember much of what was said that night. For some reason, when I think of it today, that strikes me as a terrible shame.

I'm not sure what time I awoke, but I was still mildly drunk and staggered to my room down the hall, completely forgetting to take the suitcase.

As I lay on my bed, I felt a strange anxiety take hold. It seemed to suddenly occur to me that our chances of getting the heroin through to Australia were extremely remote, considering all the warning signs that had thrown themselves in our path. In a moment of clarity, I knew the best thing to do was wash the heroin down the bathtub. I raised myself from my bed to do this, but then realised the suitcase was still in Paul's room. And in that fateful one second of my life, I decided to lie back down and give the matter more thought. I turned my head to look at the clock. It was 8.30 a.m.

In minutes I had fallen back into an uneasy asleep, where I dreamed I was being pursued by something harmful. I was running through a forest, my feet crunching on the brown autumn leaves that carpeted the floor of the wood, and although I could not see my pursuer, I could hear and feel it. It was something wicked and it was hunting me. I screamed out as I ran, but no voice came from my mouth. Suddenly I entered a clearing, and in the middle of this clearing was a monolithic statue of a bearded man sitting on a throne, staring straight ahead. In his right hand he held a trident, but I could see the middle prong was missing.

I stood motionless before this statue, in awe of it. I then heard my pursuer enter the clearing and, just as I thought it would be upon me, it stopped too. I slowly turned my head to see, but, just as the shadow of the hunter began to come into view, I awoke.

Somebody was knocking at the door.

CHAPTER 4

HELL

9.00 a.m., Wednesday, 11 October 1978.

MAJOR VYRAJ ANNOUNCES himself as an immigration official, and for a moment I relax. My body is stunned back into a state of panic by a crunch to my stomach from his walkie-talkie. I collapse on the floor and know that my life and the world it lives in is suddenly, horribly out of my control.

Thai policemen carrying guns are tearing the room apart, babbling things I cannot understand. There is shouting from somewhere else in the hotel and I am dragged by both arms out into the hallway and down to Paul's room. He is being pressed against the wall with guns at his head while other policemen are standing over the red suitcase. They urgently chorus something toward Vyraj and he squeezes my face till I feel my cheekbones will break.

'This suitcase has a coded lock . . . tell me the number!'

I tell him the number is two-six-five and another policeman opens the lock. Insane with fear, I stupidly cling to the hope that they will close the case without looking under the flimsy blue towel that covers the 24 bags of grade-4 heroin. There is a grotesque silence in the room as the towel is removed. I want to cry but my body is so terrified it cannot manage even so simple a task. I know I am dying.

Vyraj is in a state of ecstatic rage. He marches me to the balcony and holds my head over the edge, forcing me to stare out over the bustling streets and filthy lanes below.

'See the people down there?' he barks, shaking my head like a toy. 'You can forget them now! None of them can help you! Forget about your embassy! Forget about a lawyer!'

He twists my head around until my eyes are inches from his, and from the blackness beyond I hear the words: 'Mine is the only face you are going to see for the next month!'

* * *

We are handcuffed and taken down through the hotel lobby. Incredibly, as we pass the front desk, the concierge presents us with our bill.

We are driven at high speed through the streets of Bangkok until we arrive at a large concrete building. Inside, we are told to sit and say nothing until we are spoken to. There is a table placed in front of us and the heroin is spread out on the table. Photographers arrive.

The hostility of the police is astonishing – particularly Vyraj. Though bursting with hate for us, he also appears to be having some kind of orgasm. He paces like a mad dog. I learn that he is, in fact, known by this name: 'Mad Dog' Vyraj.

He begins to shout in my face, telling me that he has been waiting for me since the beginning of the year, that he knows it was me who tried to smuggle heroin out of Thailand on a ship in February. He has been watching me since I arrived in Bangkok eight days ago. Now he has me. He says I will be shot to death by a firing squad, that he is required by law to do this to me. I don't know how to react to this news – it seems ridiculous, but the other policemen in the room do not react at all.

I declare that I want a lawyer and Mad Dog goes berserk. He screams that we have no lawyer. He screams that we have no rights at all. We are filth and are going to die. He rages as he speaks, his words fuelling his own temper. He pulls out a pistol and slams it hard upon the table.

'Do you want to die now?' he bellows. 'Do you?'

He leans toward me until, once again, his eyes are all of the world that I can see.

'You're life is worth nothing to me.'

His eyes are so black. He truly means this. He is not human. This can't be real. Every bone in my body is weakened from terror and I want to sob because my life means nothing. I can feel Paul shaking beside me. I can hear Mad Dog shouting at him but I can't hear what he's saying because I'm listening to the sound of my own fear, which is making a strange fluffy noise in my head. I wonder what my mother is doing, right at this very moment.

Mad Dog wants The Old Man. He says he knows that The Old Man is behind this affair. Both Paul and I insist that this is untrue, but Mad Dog angrily calls us liars. He says he's been watching us and The Old Man do business. He says that if we admit he is the leader, we may be charged with nothing but unlawful possession of an illegal substance and we will survive. But if we try to protect The Old Man with lies, we will be charged with collaboration for possession of heroin for the purposes of attempted export and sale. Then we will die.

Mad Dog tells us that we will be murdered under Article 27, a military law that provides for immediate execution without trial. He has murdered many drug criminals this way and will be glad to do so again. All he has to do is petition the Prime Minister of Thailand, Kriangsak Chamanand, and wait for his reply. It shouldn't be long now, for he has already sent the cable.

* * *

Mad Dog leaves the room and returns with two documents written in Thai. He places them on the table in front of us and taps on them with a thick wooden ruler with a strip of metal embedded in it. He tells us to sign them and I ask for someone to translate the documents. Mad Dog starts to laugh. He tells the other policemen what I have said and they laugh too. Then he walks behind me and stands close. He is tapping me softly on the shoulder with the ruler. He leans down toward me and I can feel his breath on my ear.

'You think you're pretty tough, don't you?'

I tell him I don't.

'Oh, yes,' he whispers. 'You like to think you're pretty tough. Yes you do. You don't want to sign this, do you? You think you're tough enough to survive in here, tough enough to survive me. Well, Mr Warren,' he sighs as he stands, 'I'll look after you.'

The rod cracks down on my head and I nearly pass out. Mad Dog pushes my head down, pressing my head into the table with all his weight.

He leaves and we are alone with the other Thai policemen. Paul and I try to talk but we are beaten whenever we make a sound or move too close to each other.

A Caucasian man enters the room with some documents. He says he is a representative from the embassy. I ask if I can see a lawyer but he says there is no need for that at this time. He begins asking questions.

'State your full name . . . What is your date of birth . . . Who is your next of kin . . .'

He seems nervous and writes very slowly. After a time, he asks us if we would like to see a priest. Paul and I are both shocked and confused by the question and ask what he means. The look on his face is one of bewilderment and he excuses himself, saying he will be right back. He is only gone for a few minutes but I can hear him speaking with Mad Dog in the room next door. Finally, he returns and sits down. He explains to us that we have been sentenced under Article 27 and are to be executed.

My gut crashes and I nearly lose control of my bowels. I am about to die. Everything I know and will ever know is about to stop.

The representative leaves the room and we are left to wait for the execution.

Mad Dog returns in a fury. He marches straight over to Paul and thrashes him, then picks him up off the floor and marches him to the door. He says something to two other policemen and they open the door to the yard outside. It is the first time we have seen sunlight in hours.

Mad Dog pulls out his gun, empties a chamber and shows us the bullet. He says it is a dum-dum bullet, which makes a small hole when it goes into the body and an enormous hole when it comes out. He says he is going to use it now on Paul. But he is a sporting man, he says, and he hears Paul is a sporting man too. He will give Paul a chance. He will let him run for 100 yards before he shoots. If he misses, Paul is free. If he doesn't miss, then he will say that Paul tried to escape. Mad Dog says it is more than a fair deal, as we are both going to die anyway.

Paul will not do it. Mad Dog brings his pistol down hard onto the back of Paul's neck and pushes him into the open doorway. He says that if Paul does not run, he will shoot him dead right there where he stands. He levels the gun at the side of Paul's head and cocks it. At the sound of the cocking hammer, Paul's body jerks and lurches backwards, but Mad Dog pushes him again into the doorway. Paul struggles backwards and in a flash the other policemen are shouting at him and pushing him back out into the sunshine. The shouting and struggling goes on for an eternity and Paul is becoming terrified and violent. I know that he is about to be killed.

I can't take this any more. And I shout out that I will sign the document.

* * *

The Old Man is marched in. He glares at us with contempt as Mad Dog tells him that we have implicated him as the leader. The Old Man furiously protests his innocence. He tries to use his usual suave air and I can see that it is throwing Mad Dog into a murderous mood. But there are more policemen present now – some high-ranking Thais and a few officials from the Australian embassy – and violence will not be tolerated.

It is now very late in the evening and, after a time, we are placed in chains and led outside to where a bus is waiting to take us to the police cells not far way. The Old Man is separated from Paul and I, no doubt to keep us from collaborating our stories.

There are no beds in the cells. Somehow, I manage to sleep. I don't have any bad dreams. I don't need them.

* * *

Every morning they come at 6.30 and take us to the police interrogation cells at the Drug Suppression Unit. We return at eight or nine at night. Sometimes there are embassy representatives present and Mad Dog cannot hurt us physically, so he breaks us emotionally. He is quite brilliant. He talks endlessly, repeating over and over that our lives are worth nothing and I believe it. In the madness, I realise I am actually respecting him as an interrogator. I keep forgetting that this must be part of his psychological strategy.

We are told that he has compiled a 200-page document which has been sent to the Prime Minister – a further, more vehement request for our immediate execution. We no longer know whether this will be going ahead today or whether it is a reality at all. To live with this spectre from one hour to the next is insanity.

There are more documents Mad Dog wants us to sign. Day after day he uses everything in his power to get us to do what he wants. One morning, he proceeds to tap me in the leg with the toe of his boot. The blows are weak, but they continue for hours. When I go to stand at the end of the day, I collapse. The muscle in my leg has been crushed.

* * *

One morning, as we lie in our cells, a newspaper is pushed under the door. The *Bangkok Post*. The front page features two photos: one of a miserable-looking man being carried to the execution chamber; the other shows the chamber from the same angle, only now a coffin is being carried out. It is flanked by two praying monks. The caption underneath the two photos tells of how the executioner will be using his gun again very soon – for the three Australians arrested recently in Bangkok. Paul and I are emotionally exhausted. We can take no more of this hideous existence and, after talking about it for a time, we agree that we should kill ourselves that day.

The only instrument at our disposal is a large water trough running along the wall of the cell. We decide that each will hold the other's head under the water until we are both still. We embrace each other firmly and say goodbye. It seems strange that six months ago we were strangers, yet here we are ending our lives within a few feet of each other, on a small stretch of earth hundreds of miles away from our homes.

We plunge our heads into the water, each forcing the other down with increasingly determined force. But, gradually, both of us start to resist the force of the other. After almost a minute, we simultaneously reel back out of the trough, gasping for breath. We are going to have to live through this, no matter how dreadful it becomes.

* * *

At last we are visited by a lawyer, appointed by the embassy. He tells us that it is unlikely the Prime Minister will agree to execution. By a stroke of luck, Thailand has suffered violent flooding in the north, and the Australian government has been generous with aid. It would be politically imprudent for Kriangsak Chamanand to slaughter any Australians right now. We will have a trial.

Mad Dog is not happy about this and finds he must resort to stronger tactics to bend our spirit. One morning, he tells me he has something to show me and marches me down to the bathroom at the end of the interrogation room. Inside, I see a Thai prisoner in heavy chains, standing in a tub of water. He has what appear to be electric wires running between his nipples and his genitals. Mad Dog has another policeman attach the two wires to a large battery. The Thai prisoner howls in pain and collapses into the water, where he begins to thrash about like a fish. Like some sort of insane artist, Mad Dog turns to see how I am admiring his work. He tells me this will happen to me too unless I comply with him . . .

* * *

We are awoken one morning to be told that we are being moved from the police cells. The interrogation is over. We are going to court to be formally charged and then taken from there to a prison. I am frightened of going to a Thai prison – I've heard they are despicable places. But right now I am simply relieved to be away from Mad Dog and this torment.

My relief disintegrates when I hear the voice of a jeering Thai guard.

'Ha, ha, ha . . . you go Monkey House!'

CHAPTER 5

MONKEY HOUSE

NOTHING ANYONE CAN do to me will ever compare to those 37 days of interrogation. It lives on in my head and actually makes me feel sick with fear when I think of it. It was just so fucking terrifying. People think that criminals are hardened to such experiences, and some might be to a degree. But I was a courier. I never had to look at the damage I may have inflicted. Mentally, I wasn't terribly different from the ordinary working-class man. Violence, hatred, torture, constant fear of immediate death – these were not things I'd had to deal with on a day-to-day basis. Yet there we were, being assaulted by all four at once, in a confined space, from dawn till dusk for 37 days. That will change you. The rest of my time in Thailand would change me further still. But it really began in those 37 days. Any of you – and I know you are many – who hate me and believe that I deserved to die, well, there's a big concrete building in Bangkok called the Police Interrogation Unit. The Warren Fellows of 1978 went in and will never come out. That makes it a grave. You are welcome to spit on it.

* * *

Once released from our cells, I was introduced to a new sensation which would play a big role in my life for the next decade: chains. These chains were enormous and were to be fixed to my ankles by a blacksmith with an anvil and hammer. I was ordered to lift my leg up onto the anvil, whereupon the blacksmith joined two heavy, semi-circular bands of iron around the bone, hammering a bolt through the clasp, like a cufflink. Both ankles were secured in this way, then joined together by another chain. Walking was terribly difficult. Particularly, as I was to discover sometime later, when the blacksmith thought you'd looked at him the wrong way.

* * *

Outside the courtroom there was a frightening crowd of reporters and photographers. I'd no idea we'd become such big news. They seemed to be most interested in Paul. What a pity. In all his career as a champion sportsman he'd never received such attention.

In court, we signed our charge papers – written entirely in Thai – and were informed that it was yet to be decided whether we would receive a trial or execution. By this point, the relentless threats of death had become strangely dull.

Just before dusk, we were escorted outside, where a ragged truck was waiting for us. We were told we were being taken to Bumbud, a remand and reform prison solely for drug cases. The truck had a large cage on the back, into which we and many other prisoners were herded by guards using electric cattle prods. We moved as quickly as we could, but it didn't matter – we all got a jolt. The guards were allowed to use them and so they simply did.

We were driven through the bustling streets of Bangkok like animals in a circus parade – anyone who wanted to watch or wave or laugh could do so.

Considering everything I'd already been through, I don't know why I found this so terrible. It just seemed that after all the torture and terror and loneliness of the last month, public humiliation was the final knife in the heart. When you've been stripped of everything, and all you have left is one last shred of pride, you can't handle it being mocked.

It was dark when we reached Bumbud. The entrance doors we had to walk through were huge and made of iron. It seemed like something out of the Dark Ages. The place looked desolate and angry.

Once inside, we were made to stand in line with the few possessions we had been allowed to carry. All money was to be confiscated. We were ordered to strip and were ruthlessly searched by guards. All but the guards were silent throughout the whole processing ordeal. It seemed odd to me that they made us sign admittance forms, as if we were giving our permission, consenting, of our own free will, to this whole ordeal and our entrance into a dungeon.

We were asked if we wanted to eat. I was so starving hungry I thought I could have eaten anything. But when I saw what was offered – three plates of rice on the ground with a dirty liquid that looked like it might be some kind of stagnant soup – I began to lose my appetite immediately. I forced myself to taste this, praying that it might not be as disgusting as it looked. It was dreadful, and I couldn't swallow any more than a mouthful.

We were then told that we were to sleep now. I began to realise that imprisonment in these places was total and without relief. Ordered to shower, ordered to eat, ordered to sleep before 8.30 p.m., with all orders, no matter how small, delivered with a hint of abuse. It was like being a hated child in a hard boarding home.

I often hear people talking about how prisoners have it easy inside: they have televisions and live in 'luxury'. The thing people don't realise is that it is not appliances and simple comforts that give people their freedom, but the ability to exercise options. To eat when you want to, shower when you want to, go for a walk or talk to a particular person late at night. These are the things you really notice when they are taken away from you. Your freedom to make decisions based on what you want is the only thing that sets you apart from an animal in a zoo. To have this taken from you by some person you've never seen before and who, really, has no more of a moral right than you to act on his personal dislike for you, seems just too outrageous to bear. And this prison – these vaults in Thailand – are the most notorious robbers of human dignity in the world.

We were herded upstairs to our sleeping quarters, where I was totally crushed by what I saw. One room, about the size of a small, rectangular swimming pool, for about 30 of us. There were no beds – just straw mats on the floor – and the prisoners were, quite literally, shoulder to shoulder. Every man was sweating profusely and the stench was sickening. There seemed to be no air in the space that surrounded their writhing bodies – just vile-smelling, ugly space. A fluorescent light hummed above us constantly. I don't recall if I slept. I must have. I can't possibly imagine what I would've been thinking to myself had I stayed awake all night.

I do know that I cried that night in the Monkey House. And I would only cry twice again during my time in Bangkok. Somehow, by the time morning arrived, I had forgotten how to cry.

* * *

In the morning we were taken downstairs for a bath. This consisted of stripping naked and splashing ourselves with water from a horse trough. The water itself was filthy, siphoned from a nearby river which was full of excrement and rotting carcasses of animals. And it was here that I saw, for the first time, the sadistic brutality of the guards, particularly towards other Thais. Each of the guards carried a hard bamboo cane which was used freely and without any sign of inhibition or restraint. One Thai prisoner – and I have no idea what he did – was beaten so badly that his naked flesh had weeping, cracked wounds all over it by the time he was ordered to put his clothes on again. We were then taken back upstairs for more questioning. I don't understand what these questions were in aid of, for they were repetitive in the extreme.

Paul, The Old Man and I were then sent to Building Four, where most of the prisoners were foreigners. I had hoped that this would be an improvement on the standard of the previous evening, but it was not to be. Our room, although containing fewer prisoners, was much smaller. In the corner of the room was a hole in the floor which served as a toilet. Everything that came out of your body went into this hole, which was cleaned and emptied infrequently. The room was stifling.

All of the 24 men in that room were in there for drug offences. And all of them were using heroin. I was astonished. I'd just seen a Thai prisoner nearly killed for something trifling, and here were all these foreigners taking drugs. I soon discovered that drugs were quite available in Bumbud. Anything was available if you had money. Our money had been confiscated when we arrived, but, in one of the few displays of consideration by this system, the money had been placed in our own personal prison accounts, from which we were given small amounts upon request. Also in Building Four was a small food store which sold eggs, bread, tins of fish, canned milk and white rice. We could cook this up on a small spiral of electric wire which was positioned in the corner of our room. That was about as luxurious as things got. Unless you used and could buy heroin.

* * *

We were soon visited by our lawyers. Mine was a young Thai, who told me that a date had been set for our trial. I was relieved that the dreaded Article 27 had not been invoked, but I was also aware that the penalty we received would probably be life.

Life. In this place. I wondered if I would ever get used to it. It seemed as impossible to imagine as death.

Not long after this, Paul, The Old Man and I heard from a Chinese prisoner that one of the Thai guards could be bribed to assist in an escape plan. This was certainly the most exciting news we'd heard since our arrest, and further investigation seemed to show the rumour was sound. We had noticed that escape seemed relatively easy – head counts were taken infrequently and all one had to do was find a way over the wall of the yard. It looked a little dicey, but the idea of it working out seemed too attractive to pass up.

The next time we were visited by our lawyers I mentioned to one of them – an Englishwoman who seemed particularly trustworthy and sympathetic towards our cause – that I needed $10,000 fairly urgently. She seemed to work out pretty smartly what I was up to and said she'd see what she could do. I also asked her to contact my family in Australia and inform them that everything would be all right soon and not to worry.

The following day, the three of us were marched into the governor's office. The English lawyer who had seemed particularly trustworthy and sympathetic to our cause had gone straight to prison officials with news that we were planning an escape. Apparently, she had done so for our own good, as she believed we would surely have been shot.

The governor was furious and demanded that we all be put in heavy chains. This was carried out almost immediately, with the prison blacksmith ensuring the odd error of judgement was made.

No sooner had we been placed in chains – chains far heavier than those we had worn earlier – than we were informed we were being moved immediately to another prison. A prison with higher security. A prison called Maha Chai.

I had heard of a game once played in Maha Chai – a game that had gone on to become something of a legend. I never saw this happen myself, but I saw drawings the other prisoners had done that depicted the game. The guards would build a ball out of thatched bamboo, just big enough for a small human being to be placed inside. There was a hatch with a lock on the outside. On the day the game was to be played, some unpopular Thai prisoner was brought to the yard and placed inside the ball. The guards would push the ball around for a while, just for some fun before the main event. Then, into the yard, they would lead an elephant. The elephant was going to be taught to kick the ball. As the prisoner screamed for mercy, the elephant, doing the best it could, would simply tap the ball around for a time, rolling it and its powerless inhabitant a few feet at a time. But elephants are fairly impatient animals and this would only last for a few minutes until the beast became bored. The game always ended the same way, with the elephant bringing its foot down upon the ball, crushing the man inside into a pulp of blood and bone, his last desperate howls buried by the laughter of the guards.

CHAPTER 6

THE FUN FACTORY

THE MERE MENTION of Maha Chai gave foreigners nightmares, especially those that had been there before. It was said that Maha Chai was sadistic and cruel, and the stories I'd heard were frightening. I'd heard about things called darkrooms: tiny cells with no light where prisoners would be locked for months. Few, it was said, came out alive.

Maha Chai was an old wooden monolith built by the French almost 100 years ago. There were multiple gates and walls so escape appeared to be completely impossible. Nevertheless, we were informed – to our horror – that because we had now proved ourselves to be such a bad security risk, we would be shackled like animals every day. It seemed unbelievable that these chains, so rusty and dirty and already eating into my ankles, would not be off my feet at any time that I might be able to walk. Paul and I could barely perform the simplest standing movement. We soon learned that it was possible to bribe the blacksmith, with either money or cigarettes, to loosen the shackles a little. We also learned, how-ever, that the guards could bribe the blacksmith too. Every day when the chains were adjusted or checked, the blacksmith would bring his hammer down. You had no way of knowing whether the guard had asked him to hit or miss. I saw many ankles broken in this way, with prisoners screaming with pain as the blacksmith's hammer crushed the bones that were already brittle from malnutrition. This was just the beginning of the mental torture that made Maha Chai notorious.

We were processed and placed in a tiny room which stank of wounds. The people in here were so badly treated. They were beaten and left to rot. We soon discovered that we'd spend 18 hours a day in our rooms, which sometimes were packed with up to 30 prisoners. There was a hole in the corner of the room which served as a toilet, and was supposed to be emptied and cleaned every three days. Next to the toilet was a bowl of water, as toilet paper was not allowed in the prison. After several days of use, the entire cell was so thick with the smell of excrement that there was scarcely any point in using the toilet. It was simple to contract diarrhoea, so you can imagine the squalor that the cell would become after several days without cleaning, and they hardly ever cleaned. If a prisoner lost control of himself in his sleep, there would almost certainly be a fight. The Thais had procured knives in here and apparently the fights were bloody and often deadly. Maha Chai was a cesspit of blood and excrement and death and cruelty.

* * *

It was Building Two that the prisoners feared most. Building Two was the punishment building, and it housed some of the darkrooms. These were rooms big enough for about ten people to live in very uncomfortably – there were usually about 20 prisoners in one room at a time. It was said that absolutely no sunlight penetrated the blackness of the darkrooms. Prisoners were allowed out for five minutes in the morning, to eat inedible food and wash. The usual bucket was in the corner and it was never emptied. No matter what crime you had committed to deserve a stretch in the darkroom, the minimum sentence of one month applied. And you were in there for 23 hours and 55 minutes a day. The five minutes in the morning to wash and eat were the highlight of the day. The rest of the time, they simply did not open the door. Sometimes, prisoners would be in darkrooms for up to three months. Three months without light, medical attention, decent food or any semblance of hygiene. The prison authorities denied there were darkrooms. It was common knowledge that if you committed certain acts, you'd do time in the darkrooms, but signs would come down if any embassy members or Thai authorities visited: 'There are no such things as darkrooms in this prison.' The sadistic governor knew that the authorities would consider the darkrooms inhumane, even for criminals, and he was desperate to keep them going. Most people who went to the darkrooms died. He liked that.

* * *

Another aspect of Maha Chai which added to the misery was the wildlife. There were cockroaches everywhere, crawling in everything and disturbing any sleep that you managed to get. During the day, the heat would bring ants out of the woodwork and, if you lay still for a while, they'd take to you. At night, the mosquitoes were persistent. The Thai airforce. Everything that lived in this place seemed bent on attack.

But the most horrifying of all were the sewer rats. As large as small cats, they were easily the ugliest, most frightening animals I've ever seen. They had long snouts like anteaters, fangs and wicked eyes that seemed to glow in the dark. Their bodies were thick and slimy, as if oozing some sort of oily sludge. They weren't shy and retiring, like rodents back in the cities of Australia, but were vicious and fearless. They actually hissed at you when you looked at them. If you've ever seen those Warner Bros cartoons where a woman jumps on a chair at the sight of a mouse, you'll know something of how 30 hardened criminals looked when one of these rats got into a room. They'd come out at night in little packs and they'd ferociously attack, biting chunks out of you as you slept. It was dreadful. If you tried to defend yourself, say, by kicking at them, they were quick enough to take a piece out of your foot as it hit them, smart enough to go for the throat. The force of your blow wouldn't dampen their enthusiasm, but simply bring them back with a more feral determination.

One morning, Paul squatted over a hole in the floor to relieve his bowels. Out of the sewer, like something from a monster film, a sewer rat sprung and bit him on the foot. The poor bastard was inconsolable for an hour. It had nothing to do with the pain, but more the horror of the moment: being bitten by the most frightfully ugly animal in the world, which came out of the depths of a dark sewer as he was using it. Nightmarish.

It was strange to think that every single living thing in Maha Chai hated our guts.

* * *

If you've ever seen the film *From Here To Eternity*, you'll know Ernest Borgnine's character, the man who bashes Frank Sinatra. There was a guard called Prisit who looked exactly like this man, but for darker skin. He was the head officer of Building Two, the punishment wing. He wore big black Nazi-style boots and pilot's sunglasses at all times, even at night. He had a leather wristband with studs all over it, designed to break skin. He carried a big bamboo cane, the end of which was filled with concrete. He was a complete sadist. I've never known anyone who was so enthused about torture. The look on his face was always one of supreme, heartless joy.

The first time I saw Prisit in action was one morning when he stormed in and ordered many Thai prisoners out of their rooms and made them lie down on their bellies. As he walked past each prisoner, his steps slow and deliberate, he tapped his cane gently on the back of the prisoner's head. Eventually he stopped at one in particular and, tapping the prisoner's head gently with the cane, asked whether he was getting any visitors today. The prisoner, his voice quivering with fear, replied that he did not know. Prisit asked him if he had a family, and he replied that he did. Prisit then said that, next time his family came to see him, he wanted them to bring him 500 baht. The prisoner replied that he'd try, but his family was very poor and did not even have enough money to buy food for themselves to eat. Prisit then said that he didn't want to see this family of his in future unless they had 500 baht for him. For if he did, the prisoner would receive the same treatment he was about to experience. Prisit then assumed something of a combat stance over the prisoner's back and, with a spiteful ferocity I had never before seen, brought the cane biting down. The stinging sound of flesh being burned by sheer force and friction could be heard throughout the whole building, and seemed to echo for minutes.

It didn't take long for me to have my first encounter with Prisit. I was approached by a guard one afternoon and told I was to be escorted to Building Two, the punishment wing. I asked what this was for and got no reply. When I arrived in Building Two, Prisit was just strolling around in his usual tyrannical way, intimidating the motionless prisoners just by staring at them as he passed. He came to me and slowed. I was vacantly staring into his glasses, wondering if his eyes were as black as Mad Dog's. Suddenly, he turned and walked directly toward me. I glanced downward, not wanting to see. He stopped a few inches away from me and touched me gently on the chest with his right hand. His touch was so light it was terrifying. I had been told that Prisit's right arm was his favoured weapon. Ahead of any cane or boot or butt of a rifle, Prisit loved to use his right arm. My heart was exploding.

'*Chi yeng yeng*,' he whispered. '*Chi yeng yeng*,' I had heard other Thais speak this phrase to each other – it meant, 'Keep a cool heart'.

I began to feel less anxious – I had never seen him behave in such a way toward anyone and I actually sensed that he liked me. He repeated it one more time, '*Chi yeng yeng,*' his touch on my chest growing milder and milder. Then, with what scarcely seemed like a movement at all, he drove his right elbow sharply and powerfully into my solar plexus. I instantly collapsed to the floor, every skerrick of breath in my lungs having been forcibly expelled. It took me minutes to even breathe. I just sat on the floor at Prisit's feet, gasping. When I went to stand, he stamped his foot to the ground, as if to tell me that he wanted me to stay at his feet a little longer. He wanted me to know that this was the relationship he enjoyed having with me, and would enjoy for evermore.

* * *

During our first month in Maha Chai, I was constantly assured by Paul's optimism. His strength and readiness for hope was unbelievable, and he was one of the only prisoners I could see who was making an attempt to keep himself fit. Every success in his life had been obtained by challenging the odds and believing in his own chances. Though as emotionally overwhelmed as I by the dreadful position we were in, he seemed determined to triumph against the adversity. He missed his family desperately, and was crushed when his wife, Gail, gave birth to a baby daughter, just a few weeks after our arrival in Maha Chai. But where I was feeling despondent and hopeless, he never spoke of the future with bleak words. It was always 'when we get out' and 'next time I see Gail' and 'when this thing's all over'. He simply refused to believe we were finished. I loved him for that.

I, too, had been receiving letters from my family and some friends. It was strange to read them – both relieving to think that I was being thought of by those I cared for, but also terribly depressing to be reminded that life was going on outside. People I knew were walking about in the world and, when I imagined where they might be – at home in front of the television or in a favourite pub – I agonised over the fact that I'd probably never join them, or even be able to look upon the scene of them just living. Never again. I felt as if I were locked not just in a prison, but in a bubble that time had forgotten and was rolling past in waves.

One letter that made me very upset came from my mother. Although I knew that she was desperately concerned for me, it had not occurred to me that she would be fighting her own battle. Reporters from the press had besieged the house, sometimes trying to force their way into her home. I couldn't believe it. Didn't they realise this woman would be distraught that her son was in terrible trouble? Didn't they have the compassion to leave her alone? She couldn't even so much as step out to go to the shops without being set upon by people asking questions she simply had no answer for. I became heavy with the thought that I had made my poor mother a prisoner too.

Another letter which was to affect me was one I received from a friend in Australia. In the letter, she told me that she had seen the film *Midnight Express*, the true story of Billy Hayes, who was arrested for drug trafficking in Turkey and was brutalised by the harsh conditions of the prison. My friend wrote to tell me that she now understood what I might be going through. But this was a letter I was never to read.

* * *

One morning, the guards took me from my cell and, without explanation, began marching me towards Building One. Desperate with fear, I begged them to tell me what was happening. One of them told me I was going to the darkroom.

I was petrified. I had scarcely been in this prison for a few weeks and had been too frightened to do anything wrong at all, yet I was being sent to the place of supreme punishment. No amount of protesting could alter the situation, and within minutes I found myself locked in the tiny, stinking room with at least 20 other strangers.

The first few minutes were horrifying. We were so cramped that we all had to crouch against the wall, and there was not even enough room for all of us to stretch our legs out in front of our bodies. We were all wearing chains. The combined smell of us was terrible. The room smelled so bad that several prisoners were sick and many were crying. As the mass of bodies jostled for space and some sort of comfort, I remembered that those thrown into the darkroom would usually be inside for at least a month. I seriously doubted I would survive a day of this.

After what seemed hours of bitter physical and emotional distress for us all, a strange sense of understanding seemed to develop among those of us cramped in this miniature prison. Although we couldn't converse in the same language, or even see each other very well at all, we seemed to be communicating as a group. The message being sent was remarkably clear: we were not to fight amongst ourselves, for that was what the guards and the prison system wanted. We had to try to survive together, for if one did not cope, then all would not. Nobody wanted to hurt. Most of the Thais in here were going to be executed, and life was now precious to them, even if it was degrading.

We all knew that any anxiety or argument would kill us all. We were each part of a horrible mass that had to run a motionless marathon together, and as a group we could survive. We began giving each other room, taking shifts in which we could stretch our legs while the prisoner opposite drew his own to his chest. There was no talking. There was nothing to say. We tried so hard.

This made the darkroom more tolerable than it might have been, but it was still appallingly uncomfortable. Every moment was a stretch of endurance, and there was no way of simply closing my eyes and imagining some dreamy thought from miles away. The reality of this painful physical situation was so immediate that it was just impossible to wander off into my imagination, the only place where I might normally escape. If, by some miracle, I did manage to become momentarily accustomed to my twisted position against the hard walls, the cockroaches would soon bring me back. It was hideous. We were being forced to think of our torture every moment, every day. That is what they wanted us to do.

* * *

In the morning after one of the longest nights I will ever endure, a shaft of light penetrated the gloom that had swallowed this place for so long. There were cracks in the ceiling of the darkroom, just big enough to let some air in to circulate around the upper reaches of the room. Through these openings, a brief ray of light pierced suddenly through the blackness, like some sort of holy curtain. After so much dark, it was almost a beautiful sight. It was only visible for a few moments, however, before fading away, as if it had not seen anything inside the darkroom that it wanted to look at for long.

The door of the darkroom was abruptly opened. A whistle blew and we were ordered, all of us, out of the cell. It was time for us to wash. There was barely any light in Building One at all, but what light there was still hurt my eyes – the darkroom had been pitch black.

All of our movements were to be made at the sound of the guard's whistle. When it blew, we lurched a few feet forward, our chains dragging on the floor underneath us. The whistle blew again, and we picked up the soap to lather ourselves until, a few seconds later, the whistle blew again, telling us to stop. Somebody hadn't stopped quick enough and was instantly caned on the back. At the sound of the whistle, we staggered forward again, toward small bowls of water on the floor. We were to wash the soap off our bodies with no more than three bowls of water. Water had to be conserved, they said, for others in the prison to drink. The whistle blew again and we picked up the bowls and began to trickle the water over our dirty, soapy bodies. Before I knew it, I'd used my three bowls of water and was still covered in a thick lather of brown soap, which was already becoming sticky from the heat. I reached for another bowl out of sheer instinct – to wash such stuff from my body was an action I had performed for 25 years without a thought. My natural instincts were brought back screaming to the reality of Maha Chai as the stinging crack from a cane lashed at my back. In pain, I dropped the bowl and the remaining water within it. The cane bit into me again and I was hauled away from the bowls of water by a yelling guard.

We were marched to a table for breakfast which, of course, was inedible. Dirty rice. I tried to eat some of it, but not even my hunger could force me to do so.

The whistle blew and we lurched back and the whistle blew again and we were back in the darkroom and the door was closed shut. There I would sit, with a dirty film of soap being baked into my skin by the furnace-like heat of the darkroom, until the whistle blew again the following morning.

* * *

The wooden bucket that served as the toilet for 20 of us, many with dysentery, remained in its spot in the corner, unemptied now for a day and two nights. The heat seemed to cause the smell to move into our bodies instead of simply around them, so that placing cupped hands over my mouth and nose was no help. The air from my lungs was the same fetid air that lived in this room.

* * *

After several days, I was thirsty and hungry beyond belief. I couldn't believe I was in this hole in the earth and I couldn't believe I was surviving it. I still didn't know why I was here, and all requests for an explanation were met with a barked order to be quiet and follow the sound of the whistle.

One morning, after returning from breakfast and wash, I noticed that some of the Thai prisoners had taken their rice and, rather than eating it themselves, had managed to smuggle it back to the darkroom. I couldn't imagine what they were planning on doing with it, but felt sure that it was bound to be more interesting than whatever was happening in the Maha Chai breakfast kitchen. I managed to struggle my way over to the far side of the darkroom, where the Thais seemed to be preparing something. As I got closer, I saw that one of them was lifting a loose board from the floor. Peering into the blackness, I noticed the ground below the floor seemed to be moving. The Thai began to empty the rice down into the moving mass. It took a few seconds for the scene to register: underneath the floorboards was a teeming body of the biggest cockroaches I had ever seen. And the Thais were feeding them, fattening them up to eat.

One of them scooped down with a plastic bag and hauled to the surface a large catch of these fat bugs, scuttling around in the bag, falling over each other, much like us. The Thais then began fiddling with empty milk and food cans that had been hidden under the floorboards too. The bugs were then pressed into the cans and pulped into mash. Another Thai had secured a small amount of oil, which went into the mix. Another had some salt.

One of the Thais noticed me watching and offered me some of the dish, but I refused. I couldn't possibly eat this, no matter how hungry I was. In broken English, he insisted that I eat, that this was the only source of protein I would get in this place. Without it, he said, I would wither away and die. I tried to explain to him that, where I come from, those bugs were considered to be the filthiest creatures of all. He told me that was the very reason that so few foreigners survived the darkrooms of Maha Chai.

Reluctantly, I ate.

* * *

After a few days, I finally learned to sleep in the darkroom. I began to have dreams that I was home, doing ordinary, almost mundane things. No matter how commonplace the activity played out in my dream was, it was always presented in the finest detail. I'd see and sense everything exactly as it would be: the steam rising from a freshly made cup of morning coffee; the sound of a breeze in my ear on a warm afternoon; the smell of freshly cut grass or new books in a bookstore. Sometimes, the dreams would play back real events from my life as a free man: the bandits who stopped our bus in Bogota, Colombia, armed with rifles and belts of shells, just like the Mexican bandits in western movies; the one-eyed Indian man playing cards by the dock in Bombay, as his friend showed me rooms filled with hashish; and Avril. Often I'd awake from these dreams and, for just a moment, wonder where I was, believing myself to still be in the world I'd just come from. Then I'd remember.

One night, I dreamed of something else I'd seen in India. Walking along a road near the water, I saw a young girl struggling to her feet. She wasn't dressed like a street dweller, but seemed very ill and in a desperate state. I asked Richard what was wrong with her and he said she was a heroin addict. That day, I'd made a little deal with God: I told him that if I ever got involved with heroin in my life, he must destroy me.

After almost a week, I managed – through a benevolent guard – to get a request to the prison governor. I wanted to know why I was in this place. I didn't understand it at all. I was heartened to hear that Paul had also been making inquiries on my behalf. There had been some talk in the prison as to why the relatively new foreign prisoner had been sent to such a place. Later in the day, a guard opened the door of the darkroom and escorted me to the governor's office.

In the governor's hand was a letter. He told me that the prison officials had read the letter – as they do with all incoming mail – and were convinced it contained a coded message about my future escape attempt. I told the governor this was nonsense, that I had only been in Maha Chai for a short time and had not yet even been able to plan my survival within its walls, let alone plan an escape. He asked me, then, to explain exactly what the term 'Midnight Express' was supposed to refer to.

I told him that it was a popular film in our country, and that if somebody had mentioned it in a letter to me, they would simply have been saying that they had seen it and perhaps were identifying with my predicament.

At this, the governor seemed unconvinced. He told me he'd think about it and I was promptly marched back to the darkroom.

Sent to the darkroom because a friend of mine had seen a film and written to me about it. I would have to write to everyone I knew, to warn them of the dangers that lay for me in the slightest suspicious phrase.

In the meantime, there was nothing else to do but sit and wait and pray that none of my friends back home would bother going to see *Escape From Alcatraz*.

* * *

For days one of the Thais had been taking out a large nail at regular intervals and sharpening it on a rock. At first, I hadn't taken much notice of this, convinced it was simply his way of passing the time. But I noticed some of the other Thais were becoming a little edgy about him. This was the sort of thing that we didn't need in this place. The anxiety would breed like the cockroaches under the floorboards. I tried to forget about the man with his nail, but the sharpening sound began to alarm me. I tried to think of it as like the ticking of a clock. That worked for a time.

Later that day there was something of an incident. A fluttering sound was heard from above, toward the roof of the darkroom. We all looked upwards and saw it together: a white bird, sitting at the edge of the crack in the ceiling and peering in, as if it had some business with us that it felt it had to attend to. It was tremendous to see this bird. After days of nothingness, I would have been able to stare at it for hours and it would have almost made this place bearable. The bird made a noise, just one small rasp. Then, of course, it lost interest and flew away. It had better things to do.

The Thais were somewhat alarmed at this sight. Being superstitious by nature, they were convinced it was some sort of sign. To them, visions such as this always carried a message, especially with birds involved. Apparently, some of them believed it was a message of death.

* * *

I was almost asleep that night when I was sharply awakened by a scream within our cell. It was dark and almost impossible to see but somebody was attacking another. The screams became more ear-piercing and a struggle began to throw the crowded room into a state of violent chaos. The room churned around in a state of panic, our chains becoming entangled in the confusion. My eyes adjusted quickly to the dark and I could see what was happening. The man who had been sharpening the large nail was driving it again and again into the bloodied chest of another Thai, who was shrieking and choking at once. Blood sprayed around the room in geysers, splashing us all. The poor Thai struggled for his life, but the man with the nail was stabbing with such ferocity it sounded as if he were breaking bones. The terror in the room was sickening.

I had never seen anything like this and I was desperate to get away from it, but there was no escape. All we could do was boil around like a frenzied mass in this tiny slaughterhouse until the screaming had died down and the man with the nail had stopped.

A weird silence descended on the room as we all took our places by the walls that surrounded the twisted, bloodied body of the man who had been alive a few moments before. Blood was dripping from the walls where it had splashed, and a thick pool of it began to drift outwards from the body, which seemed to lie in such an unnatural position, like an insect.

I'm sure all of us wanted to alert the guards, who certainly must have heard the commotion, but nobody wanted to anger the man with the nail, who had disappeared into his own dark corner where he had worked on this for days. We just had to sit with the blood and the tension and wait for something to happen.

The hours crawled by and nobody slept. The smell of the body rose above the usual stench of the room as it leaked every fluid from inside. People had been sick everywhere. I couldn't stop thinking of how I was not meant for this, how I could not possibly live with this. I couldn't stay here. Nightmare seemed such a lame word. This was a life of total monstrosity. I wanted to die quietly in my sleep, but there was no sleep to be had.

* * *

In the morning the ray of light appeared and illuminated the atrocious scene we were living in. The guards were moving and talking outside, but were refusing to open the door.

We were in that room, with that body and the man who'd sprayed the life from it, until four o'clock in the afternoon, when the police came.

I was shifted to one of the so-called hot rooms, where the ants crawled from the sweating walls and played on my body until night fell, when mosquitoes dropped down to prick me awake.

The following morning I was awakened and told I was being sent back to Building Three. The governor believed I had been right about the film *Midnight Express*.

The previous day, a postcard had arrived for me, from my brother's wife. The picture was of a white bird in flight.

I felt like somebody or something was playing a trick on me.

* * *

I had been in that darkroom for ten days. I was still shaken by the fact that I had been sent there for such a trifling reason. Clearly, you didn't have to do too much to get there. This life was chaos.

In a moment of extreme depression – or, perhaps, courage – I decided to take an overdose of Valium. I no longer wanted to be in this place and seeing one more thing like I'd seen in the darkroom was not worth living for. Not in here. If there were some moments of real joy, I thought, it might be worth it. But not like this. In here, all opposites were negatives. The opposite to suffering was not joy, but a kind of calm sadness. The opposite to pain was not pleasure, but simply no pain. Boredom was not replaced by excitement, but fear. For me, there was nothing positive about life any more.

I managed to buy some Valium off the prison doctor, who was convinced that I was having trouble coping. I returned to my cell to take them all and stop this shit.

Paul saw me doing it and tried to stop me. But it was too late. I'd swallowed the pills and soon this whole place would be dark.

When I awoke, I remembered little of what I had done. To this day, I don't really know whether I seriously wanted to die or not. Whatever the case, Paul had apparently gone to fetch the doctor and, by the time they returned, I was already unconscious.

The incident seemed to disturb Paul more than it did me, and he begged me not to do this again. He hated it in here as much as I did, he said, but together we could get through this thing. Together, we had a chance of survival. Alone, our chances were halved.

It was obvious to me that it wasn't worth making bad friends in here. If someone wanted you dead, all they needed was $50. You give a Thai prisoner that sort of money and he'll kill you without missing a heartbeat. They could be remarkably cold-blooded. Nobody knew why that murder had occurred in the darkroom – it could have happened to anyone at any time.

I knew, then, that it would be important to make friends with the Thai prisoners, or at least understand them. As a general rule, it appeared that the particular races stuck together: Thai with Thai, French with French, Australian with Australian and Americans, naturally, with anyone who'd have them. But the Thais seemed to be the masters here. They controlled by weight of numbers. Thais treated foreigners with a similar sort of respect to that which their free countrymen are famous for, but they were suspicious of us too. To win the trust and respect of the Thai prisoners, I had to learn their language as best I could.

During the many long days sitting in the crowded yard of Maha Chai prison, I did my best to try to converse with as many Thais as possible, learning a phrase here and there. Most of them came from families so poor that they were getting absolutely no money from the outside, and so were forced to work for other prisoners, washing clothes and such. I had a decent supply of money coming in from family and friends, so I took the opportunity to employ their services whenever I could. I began to get comfortable with their way of thinking.

Almost the entire Thai culture seems to be based around myths or legends. Their language is incredibly descriptive and they explain everything through imagery and symbolism. They are fascinated by the spirituality of animals, and almost everything they see reflects this. Their bodies may carry tattoos, usually of a dragon or some kind of bird. In many ways, this sums up their national character perfectly. They are survivors by nature, with the patience to endure almost anything if they believe it will serve a greater good in the long term. But their temperament can crack with the unpredictability of a caged tiger.

As I have mentioned, Thais are also deeply superstitious – northern Thais in particular – but it's hard to dismiss this as stupidity. Some of them seemed to have remarkable healing powers. I saw many Thais exercising mind over body in such a way that nothing seemed to be able to pierce their skin. A bamboo cane would just break in two. Once, I saw a Thai sitting in his cell, his eyes closed as if he were far away, throwing water over himself. He sat there for days in this upright position, not moving at all. Later, when I saw him in the yard, I asked what he had been doing for all of this time. He replied that he had been to visit his village. He had seen his family and all of his friends and he was now happy to soldier on in Maha Chai until he visited them again. Seeing my look of bewilderment, he smiled and told me that I couldn't possibly understand, that I didn't understand the power of the spirit like he did.

After some of the strangeness I'd encountered in the last few years, I was beginning to have a lot of respect for Thai people.

* * *

I was approached one morning and told that I had a visitor who was not a lawyer. I got very excited wondering who it might be . . . until I saw that it was The Old Man's son. I had met him once or twice in the years before my arrest and, although I got on well with him then, I knew why he was here now. He wanted to know why I had signed a statement saying his father was responsible for the heroin shipment when I knew full well that he wasn't. I felt deeply sorry for him. He was both angry and very distressed. I explained how the Thai police seemed to want to arrest The Old Man for this no matter what, and that they had threatened myself and Paul with all sorts of torture if we did not sign statements saying that he masterminded the whole affair. At first, Old Man Junior didn't believe me, but when I told him about Mad Dog giving Paul 100 yards to run, he seemed to think that the story was too horrible for me to have made up. He begged me to testify about this in court. He didn't care whether I liked his father or not, it was a matter of the gravest principle. He said he thought it was a tragedy that I had wound up in this hideous place, but, if The Old Man was innocent of this crime, it was a more woeful tragedy that he should be here as well.

I saw his point and, even though I was frightened of confronting Mad Dog again in court, I agreed to write a statement which could be tendered as evidence. While Old Man Junior waited outside, I returned to my cell and, after bribing a guard to wait, I began writing. I wrote that I was making the statement of my own free will and was not being threatened or harassed by The Old Man. I told of how I had signed the statement implicating The Old Man out of fear for my personal safety, and that he had nothing to do with the crime he had been incarcerated for. I told of how it was wrong that he had been imprisoned with me and that I hoped he would soon be freed from this prison. This part I wrote with real conviction. I then gave the note to the guard to take to Old Man Junior.

I did seriously hope that The Old Man would get out. He was, as I have said, not guilty of this particular crime. And, for once, I found myself feeling a little sorry for him. He was still trying to affect that suave rubbish and it just wasn't washing with anyone. You could see The Old Man's whole persona cracking apart under pressure. But the real reason why I wanted to see him go was that he was becoming a top-stripe pain in the arse. He cried all the time – and I certainly don't blame him for that – but he also complained about things to the prison guards or officials, as if he were in a hotel and was not getting the service he had paid for. To me, and anyone with any sensitivity at all, this place was so abhorrent and the conditions so disgusting that there was no place to start as far as complaining was concerned. There was simply so much wrong with life in here that trying to change anything was farcical.

* * *

After some months, our trial began. We were very heavily chained and driven to court in an old bus. From the first day of the preliminary hearing, it was clear the whole thing would be a ridiculous waste of everyone's time. There was no jury, no stenographer, none of the trappings of a modern court of law. All that was there to represent the mighty wheels of justice was one judge who, as our lawyers delivered their addresses, never looked up from his notepad, on which he appeared to be simply doodling with a pencil.

I returned to Maha Chai clearer than ever in the knowledge that this was now my home.

* * *

One night I was awakened by another screaming prisoner in our cell. Startled, I jumped up and searched the room. I was relieved to see that it was simply one of the newer prisoners having a nightmare. Eventually, whatever horrible vision it was drifted away, and the man continued to sleep. Over the next few nights, however, this same scream would rise up from his throat, almost always at the same time of night and lasting for the same few minutes.

One morning, I approached the man to talk. At first, we could not communicate at all, for he was Cambodian and could not speak a lot of English. But he seemed keen to talk to somebody, so I found someone who knew both our languages and, through him, I learned the Cambodian's story.

His name was Hou. He had lived on the outskirts of a small

country village in central Cambodia, with his mother, father and sister. Like many from that region, his family were very poor, but together they led a peaceful existence. His sister was very pretty and it was hoped she would marry into wealth some day.

One afternoon, Hou made his daily journey to the nearby river to bring water back to the home. It was a mild day and so he took the time to sit on the riverbank for a while, listening to the splash of the river's tiny rapids. Perhaps half-an-hour had passed before he stood, collected some water in his containers and began to make his way home. In the distance, he noticed a cloud of black smoke rising from the very area where his family had their home. He began to run, making sure not to lose any water from the buckets, as it might be needed.

But when he got close enough to see, he realised it was much more than a fire. He could hear his sister crying out as if in agony. There were about six soldiers, wearing the uniforms of the Khmer Rouge, standing in front of the house with their weapons over their shoulders. Hou instinctively dropped out of sight, taking refuge in the long grass. And from here he watched the scene that was to make him scream in his sleep every night for years.

His father was kneeling on the ground, his sister and mother being held down lower in the grass. Hou raised his head slightly and saw that his sister had her clothes torn from her and was being savagely raped by two of the soldiers. As one moved away from her, another took his place. Hou saw his father stand and move to intervene, unable to take this sight any more. He was instantly shot into the ground. Hou's mother cried out in pain. One of the soldiers shot her too. Hou lay weeping helplessly, knowing that to emerge from the grass would mean the end of his life. He would stay there until the soldiers had gone, then he would try to help his sister.

He then watched as the last soldier to brutalise her stood, pulled her up by the hair and shot her in the back of the head.

This was what Hou would dream when he went to sleep at nights in his cell. While that vision stayed in his head, he told me, he would never be at peace.

And so, after witnessing the slaughter of his family, Hou now had to deal with the horrors of Maha Chai. It seemed so unfair.

But at least he only had a few years to serve. His crime was not of tremendous importance to the government of Thailand.

Hou had simply entered their country without a passport.

* * *

I saw Prisit do many dreadful things to many people. One time, he beat a Thai so heavily that the prisoner's eyes bulged from his head with blood spewing from behind them. It was as if his body had been so compressed by the beating that his inner fluids were being forced out of every possible crack in his body. On many occasions, Prisit simply caned screaming men to death.

One day, I and several other prisoners were playing a game called Hi-Lo. It involved taking the top off a Mortein can, putting two dice inside and shaking it around. While the can is being shaken, the prisoners place their bets on whether the number that emerges will be 'Hi' or 'Lo'. This may not sound to you like a sensational way to spend an afternoon, but in a place like Maha Chai, a pair of dice is like two tickets to Disneyland. Naturally, then, Hi-Lo was outlawed by the prison officials. Generally, the guards tolerated the playing of Hi-Lo. But on this particular occasion, the guard who caught us was one of Prisit's underlings.

Prisit wanted to know whose idea it was to play the game. None of us owned up. Then Prisit produced the truth serum – the bamboo cane. Still, nobody owned up. So Prisit got a better idea.

We were marched down the stairs to where a large cylinder of concrete was covered by a stone slab. Prisit ordered the other guards to remove the slab and, when they did, the stench that spewed from the depths of the cylinder was breathtaking. This was a sewage tank

– a dam where all the excrement from the building lay before being drained away. Prisit told us that it was just deep enough for a man to stand inside and have his head remain above the surface. He paused for a moment, enjoying our obvious revulsion. Then he told us to get in.

I stood motionless for a moment, convinced that he couldn't be serious. But of course he was. He could kill and torture and mangle a man. His heart would suffer no difficulty in making a man stand in shit. The dreadful odour made me retch as I climbed into the cylinder, dropping into the thick fluid until my feet hit the bottom. The movement of our bodies caused a sudden surge in the tub, which splashed the contents up over my nose and mouth. I vomited, as did the others. The level was just below my chin. We continued to be sick until the liquid beneath us changed colour. Almost as repulsive as the smell was the feeling of this broth creeping around me, seeping into every crevice and pore of my body. This was maddening and I actually moaned to Prisit to have some mercy and let us get out. And at that, he turned to his guards and told them to watch us until he returned.

It was late in the morning when we climbed into that tub. By the time Prisit returned, I had been sick so many times I was dehydrating. The muscles in my legs and neck were strained to busting point and I was feeling overcome with symptoms of poison shock. Prisit mercifully told his guards to haul us out.

It was about three o'clock in the afternoon.

* * *

I had been in Maha Chai for about six months when I received a letter from my father telling me that he was coming to visit in a few weeks. I didn't quite know how to react to this. I wanted to see my family, but I didn't want them to see me in this place. How could either of us be expected to cope?

I wrote to him saying that I'd love to see him, but under no circumstances was my mother to come too. I knew very well that she wouldn't be able to cope. She would want me to leave with her, and would not come to grips with the fact that I couldn't, that she, as my mother, didn't have more rights over my welfare than these complete strangers who didn't even speak my language. I made my father promise that he would not bring her in secret. I even contacted the embassy and begged them not to ever let her come. Please.

My father, however, did arrive. He was obviously shaken by the weight of this place, and the sight of his son peering out from within, but he held it together. Every day for two weeks he came, and after a few days conversation settled down to almost commonplace things. He told me of how the *Bangkok Post* was doing a story on him and his career as a horse trainer. It was a fine interview, he said, until the very end, when they asked the pointless question of how he felt about his son. He had no answer that they didn't know already.

This made me embarrassed, on top of everything else. I hated the thought of being an embarrassment or a humiliation for my family. I didn't dwell on that too much, though. I couldn't.

My father never bothered to ask me to tell him the truth about why I was here. Instead, he simply concentrated on how I was doing, the pending court case, whether I had friends inside the prison. That was good of him. But he had always been that way. My father was a very quiet man. He never said anything much unless he thought it definitely needed saying. He was strong and pretty wise.

Eventually the day came when he had to say goodbye. I knew this would be hard on both of us. For him, it would be difficult to leave me here in a place where, despite my best efforts to disguise it, I was desperately miserable. For me, watching my father walk out of here, knowing he was heading for the airport and home, would simply remind me, once again, that there was somewhere else that I was supposed to be, where there was a safe place kept for me.

So I suppose I should have been more prepared for the heaviness of the moment. My father broke down and wept, imploring me all the time to please, please look after myself.

I don't know how we dragged ourselves away from each other that day. I don't even think the guards could have managed to do it. Somehow, both of us chose the moment and just backed away. My father's last words to me were, 'I love you, Warren'. That was something I'd never heard him say.

It didn't occur to me at the time that I might never see my father again. A parent is somehow more aware of that possibility, but ideas like that just don't seem possible to children, even in the worst of times. What my father didn't tell me was that he already knew he was dying, and that as we waved to each other through the wire, it was the last time we would see each other again in this life.

CHAPTER 7

DRUGS

THERE WAS AN obvious abundance of drugs in Maha Chai: buddha, which the black Americans called 'cheeba', and heroin, which appeared to be used by nearly every foreigner in our building. A lot of them had never touched it before being incarcerated in Maha Chai and had only started because the conditions were so inescapably appalling.

I had now been in the hands of the hateful Thai prison system for nearly 300 days. Every waking moment had been filled with panic. Imagine the jolt of fear you feel when something shocks you while watching a horror film. Imagine that moment of fear being stretched out to last all day. That's what it was like for me. Sometimes, the despair would stop for a moment as I was distracted by some sight or comment that reminded me of something from long ago. But, very quickly, I'd feel something like an electric current burst inside me, reminding me that fear was my proper state and I must return to it. And so I took to heroin.

For anyone that has never experienced heroin, I'll do my best to describe what it feels like, not for any other reason but to explain why I became addicted to the drug in a place like Maha Chai.

There is a moment when you realise you're falling in love with someone who you know feels the same way. It has nothing to do with excitement, but more a sublime feeling of relief and deep satisfaction. Heroin is like that, only to a far greater, more noticeable physical degree. Everything seems, at worst, tolerable and fine. At best, the world is wonderful. Generally speaking, the more wretched you are feeling in a sober state, the more dazzling you'll feel when the torment is washed away by heroin. There is no feeling that your mind has been altered, as with marijuana or acid. The alteration is purely emotional – a certain feeling of synthetic happiness combined with a sense that your load has been miraculously lifted. And the heavier the load, the greater the feeling of elevation. In a place like Maha Chai – or any prison, for that matter – heroin is undeniably the perfect solution.

Naturally, coming down from this feeling is an uncomfortable realisation and you find yourself doing anything to get back to the emotional state you feel you should be in all the time. And that's the catch with this drug. While you still have the memory of the joy you have experienced, your restive state of mind will be plunged even further into the pit.

I think the authorities who try to teach children why they should avoid drugs take the wrong route by neglecting to mention that heroin itself does have a pleasant effect. All they ever tell kids is that if you use this drug you will wind up in a pool of vomit in the gutter, covered in sores and feeling like wreckage. So, when teenagers try the drug for the first time – an occurrence which is not inevitable, but more than possible these days – and they find themselves feeling indescribably terrific, with no pile of vomit or sores or feelings of hopelessness to be found, they make the obvious assumption that the authorities who warned them of such things, and neglected to mention the very real euphoria, were lying or just plain ignorant. I believe that if this surprise element was taken out of the equation there would be fewer accidental addicts.

But there was nothing accidental about my addiction to heroin. I was desperate for peace, frantically seeking some way out of the relentless misery of Maha Chai. Although our trial was approaching, I knew it was just a formality, that release was not a consideration. I believed wholeheartedly that what I was looking at here – the walls and the blank faces and the murder and the torture and the rats and the shit – was my life from now on. I just wanted to live and die here as serenely as I possibly could. I began snorting heroin and instantly felt that the situation around me was more tolerable. But snorting or smoking heroin had an obvious element of danger, as smoke could be seen or smelled by a guard and snorting could be heard. It was inevitable that I'd begin injecting.

Hypodermic syringes were not in great abundance in Maha Chai. Like everything else, you could get them if you had the money and the right guard, but for a lot the prisoners this was impossible. In this place, however, people learned to be resourceful, particularly the Thais, who are a resourceful lot to start with. They had developed a method of injection which the black American prisoners called the New York Gutter Rig.

In the absence of a syringe, they made rigs out of the insides of biros. The ink was emptied out, the insides of the biro stem cleaned as well as possible and one end burned around the finest needle that could be procured from the hospital, which was usually not very fine. The inside of the biro was then filled with the required amount and the needle forced into the vein. You had to then get someone to blow on the other end and force the heroin out.

Heroin was smuggled into the prison very easily. Bribed guards would either turn a blind eye or sell it to you themselves.

The irony here was never lost on me. The same drug that put me here was the only thing that was keeping me sane. I suppose I cannot argue with anyone who says that, at this point in time, heroin was dictating the terms of my life.

* * *

One day I was telling a joke to some of the Thai prisoners. I now had a reasonable grasp of their language, and I was pretending to call a horse race, exchanging the names of the horses with names of various prisoners and guards. They found that amusing, for some reason.

But Prisit, who happened to be passing by, did not find it amusing. His sense of humour was someplace else entirely. He didn't like the prisoners laughing at all, particularly when it was me who was telling the joke.

I had no idea why he hated me so much more than he hated others. He just did. Fortunately for me, the prison officials had somehow worked this out for themselves, and had ordered that I never be sent to Building Two, of which Prisit was the chief.

Nevertheless, he still reserved the right to make my miserable life as wretched as it could possibly be.

'You're a funny man, Warren,' he said, as the room went suddenly quiet. 'Go on, Warren. I want you to make me laugh.'

I said nothing, of course. And for my silence, I received a bashing.

Prisit then conducted a search of my things and found what he wanted: heroin. I was immediately reported and sentenced to three months in Room 39, a darkroom in Building One.

To my knowledge there were only three foreigners who ever went to the darkrooms for longer than three months and survived. I'm the only one I know of who is still alive today.

One, a German, had contracted pneumonia while inside. After his release from the darkroom, he seemed in good health, but it was probably just his emotional relief at being let out of that little box that disguised his true state of health. Before anybody realised what was happening, he simply died away.

The other, an American, was murdered by the guards. For reasons nobody knew, they just opened the door of his cell one day, grabbed him by the chains and started dragging him up and down the stairs, making sure that his head smacked into each step as they went.

They continued this for what seemed almost 20 minutes, until the screaming stopped and the man's skull had completely caved in. By the time his body appeared in the prison hospital, there were puncture marks all over his arms. The guards said that he had overdosed while climbing the stairs and had fallen, tragically striking his head as he plummeted.

Apparently, upon hearing news of her son's death, the man's mother insisted that the body undergo a full autopsy. Of course, they found no drugs in the body. I never heard about that woman again, but, if she is still alive today, she is probably still campaigning to have Maha Chai razed to the ground.

* * *

During my time in Darkroom 39, I met a Chinese prisoner by the name of Sati. Though a very gentle, spiritual man, Sati was well respected throughout the prison – by prisoners and guards alike – as a man of strong physical and mental will. It was also known that Sati was well connected on the outside.

Naturally, Prisit detested Sati, and seized every possible opportunity to break him. But, try as he might, Prisit could not make Sati show him one ounce of respect. It was well known that Prisit wanted Sati more than he wanted any other soul in Maha Chai. He was soon to get a chance.

While serving time in solitary confinement, Sati passed a note to a Thai prisoner and asked that he take it to a particular guard. The Thai said he would. On the way, however, the Thai read the note and saw that it was a request for money that friends on the outside had sent to Sati. On handing the note to the guard, the Thai said that Sati had requested the money be given to him, for safe keeping until he was released from solitary confinement.

After a few days, Sati began to inquire as to the whereabouts of his money, and eventually learned that the Thai had taken it to spend for himself. Upon release from solitary, Sati made no move to retrieve the money, and for a time it appeared as if he had forgotten the whole affair.

Months later, when Sati was doing yet another stretch in the darkroom, the Thai who had taken his note appeared. Trying to earn some extra money, he had volunteered to empty the sewer buckets from the darkrooms. As he opened the door, Sati leapt to his feet and, taking the sewer bucket in his hand, brought it crashing down upon the Thai's head, drenching him with the contents as the bucket splintered into a thousand spears of wood. Before the Thai had time to straighten himself, Sati picked up one of these splinters and, in a moment of uncharacteristic violence, swiftly thrust the spear into the Thai's ear, embedding it deeply into his brain.

Prisit wasted no time in being first on the scene – this was the moment he had been waiting for – but no guards had seen the incident occur, and nobody would have dared or even wanted to name Sati as the man responsible. Prisit was once again to be robbed of his chance to execute Sati.

Nevertheless, he dragged Sati to a punishment cell where he remained for days.

Nobody knew exactly what occurred during those few days, but we were all certain that Sati was suffering the most tormenting torture Prisit could dream up. When Sati did return to his cell, he was a physical disaster. But, as always, he sat in his corner and meditated.

Over the next few weeks, however, some noticed a change in Sati, particularly when Prisit made an appearance. Upon seeing the building chief, Sati would bow his head, not wanting to meet Prisit's gaze. But the gesture was far from humble – it seemed more contemplative, as if Sati was simply refusing to be drawn into some battle far less significant than the major storm that was approaching.

The prisoners of Maha Chai were fed up with Prisit's sadistic ego, and there were those who believed that he, having bred so much hate in so many, could not possibly be long for this world. But Prisit had his own band of lieutenants who flanked him at all times, and any attempt at assassination, even if successful, would surely end in the death of the assassin himself.

One day, a dreadful rumour began to spread through the prison. It was well known that Prisit was moonlighting as a cab driver in Bangkok. According to the rumour, Prisit was cruising the streets of Bangkok's Chinatown district – his regular beat – when he was hailed by a young Thai girl who had been out with friends. The girl was slightly drunk, and so had been chatting quite openly with Prisit. During the course of the conversation, the girl had made the mistake of mentioning that her brother, who she had loved very dearly, had died while serving a sentence in Maha Chai prison.

Prisit's black nature could not resist the gift that had just presented itself. Instead of taking the girl to her destination, he drove into a deserted laneway, raped her viciously and left her for dead in the darkened street. She was barely alive when found by a passing stranger.

This tale alarmed the Thai prisoners in Maha Chai, many of whom had families living in the city of Bangkok. For them, the implications were too shocking to bear.

One morning, sometime after this rumour began, the prisoners of Maha Chai awoke to a wave of panic that seemed to be rippling through the guards. There had been some commotion or other at the front gate. By late morning, the news of what had happened was sweeping through the prison like electricity.

The previous evening, Prisit had been working in his taxi when he was hailed by a well-dressed Chinese man who asked to be taken to a place on the outskirts of the city. It was a generous fare and Prisit would have been looking forward to a good night's takings.

When they approached the destination, however, the Chinese

man produced a gun and ordered Prisit from the vehicle. Waiting at this predetermined spot were several other men. Prisit had wandered into an ambush.

In the early hours of the following morning, the guards of Maha Chai were alerted to the presence of a figure on the road, just outside the front gate. It was Prisit, barely conscious, but alive. He had been beaten and horribly mutilated.

And his precious right hand, the one that had dealt so many blows, had been torn from its socket and placed across his chest, like the weapon of a fallen soldier.

Naturally, as this news swept through Maha Chai, the prisoners reacted with scarcely concealed glee. All except Sati.

Apparently, when informed of Prisit's fate, Sati simply smiled and nodded his head, as if hearing a story somebody had told him long ago.

* * *

The five minutes in the mornings for breakfast would sometimes become something of a scavenger hunt. If the guard was good, we might be able to do some deals for comparatively decent food. Some mornings, one of the Thais might manage to get hold of some cabbage, which he would sell to other prisoners at a sizeable profit. At other times, it might be fish. The buyer would have to somehow smuggle the food back to the darkroom to eat. Of course, when we were all so weak with hunger, the sight of another prisoner with a fish or a cabbage would be enough to spark a fight to the death.

Eating was often a difficult business. Most mornings, it was easy – there was nothing but filthy rice. One time, the guards must have decided to provide us with a little variety. When the whistle blew and we approached the bowls, we saw that as well as rice, we each had a bowl of what looked like dirty water. Upon closer inspection, I noticed the skeleton of a fish with just the head still attached, dangling in the dirty water. Like a tea-bag. The rice, too, had an added ingredient: maggots. This was not altogether unusual, as dead maggots were common in the food, along with rocks and lumps of dirt. But, this time, the maggots were alive and moving.

Many of the prisoners were so hungry they didn't even flinch, particularly the Thais, who knew how to stomach anything. One of them had once told me that anything capable of moving by itself was worth eating in Maha Chai.

But I was having trouble. I tried gulping the fish water for a while, but found it inedible. I then tried to isolate small pockets of rice where the maggots didn't seem to be populating, but they were difficult to find.

While I was concentrating on this attempt to eat, one of the guards walked by me eating a pumpkin. As he strolled passed, he spat one of the seeds into my bowl.

'*Chi yeng yeng*,' urged the Thai prisoner sitting next to me. I knew that the guard was trying to wring a reaction from me, and so I attempted to ignore it and get on with my meal. But, after strolling down the length of the line, the guard returned and spat again, this time hitting me in the face with the seed.

In an instant, the impossibility of my situation just demolished my better judgement. I leapt to my feet and hurled my bowl at him. Fortunately, it missed, but I knew nonetheless that I was in deep trouble. Without thinking, I began to run, the chains on my ankles reducing my speed to only a few lousy feet a second. I made it to the staircase before the guard was upon me, taking me by the throat and barking abuse into my face. He then marched me to the top of the stairs and into a room where I was forced to wait.

After a few moments, the guard appeared with several others. In his hand was a box of what looked like supplies. Smiling broadly, he opened the box and showed me the contents; tinned pineapple, a can of sardines, a can of baked beans and a jar of Vegemite. This parcel had come from Paul, said the guard, who had obviously received it as a gift from home. He had asked that it be put aside for me. As I sat watching, the guards proceeded to open the tins and eat. It may be unbelievable to imagine that these commonplace foodstuffs could be used as instruments of torture, but, on this particular day, being forced to watch these guards eat and laugh when I was so desperately hungry was as effective as any humiliation they could have dealt me.

Only one thing saved this scene from breaking my heart completely.

Having finished with the pineapple, the guard who had spat the seed at me proceeded to open the jar of Vegemite. Grinning, he dipped in his finger and raised a thick, gummy lump of the spread to his lips.

I was promptly returned to the cell as the guard was violently sick.

* * *

It was late at night in the middle of summer, just before the monsoon season. The summers in Thailand are wet and hot. Myself and about 20 other prisoners were packed into the cell, all of us in chains. The cell had become a sweatbox. For hours, nobody had moved – not even their mouths – as the slightest physical movement raised body temperature. Besides, there was no point in moving. There was nowhere to go to or from. And nothing to say.

Suddenly, as if he had only just appeared, a Thai prisoner lying in the corner caught my attention. He was wearing two knitted jumpers, had a blanket pulled over his body and appeared to be shivering. I stared at him for a while until I became convinced that he was ill enough for me to warrant somebody making a move. As I approached him I saw that he was perspiring so heavily it was running off his body like rain off a roof. I also became aware of a strange odour. I took the blanket off and what I saw nearly made me sick on the spot. It looked as if someone had taken a can opener, ground it around the edge of his foot and removed the sole completely. There were maggots rummaging around in his flesh and the edges of the wound were a strange colour that seemed to have no equivalent in the natural spectrum.

I called to the guard for a doctor, but he refused to do so, telling me he'd get one in the morning. I tried to insist, but the guard simply told me to be quiet and walked away.

Over the next few hours I found it impossible to sleep, for the smell of this man's wound now dominated my senses and I just couldn't ignore it. As morning approached, the other prisoners became aware of it too and had moved away from the man, leaving him sobbing and shivering in the corner alone.

Eventually, the guard opened the door and asked me whether I still wanted a doctor. While I was replying, the guard noticed the smell also and began backing away. I told him I'd carry the man if he would escort us to the hospital, to which he agreed.

As I carried the man, his eyes rolled in his head. He was clearly delirious and the smell of his perspiration was hideous. When we arrived at the hospital, the doctor took one breath and knew straightaway that the man had gangrene. He examined the man's foot and was in no doubt that it would have to be amputated. At this, the man seemed to come to his senses, declaring that he would rather the doctor take his entire life than his leg. He was Muslim, and to willingly allow any part of his body to be amputated was strictly forbidden, he said. Upon hearing this, the doctor sharply replied that he had no problem with bandaging the man and allowing him to lie down on a hospital bed and die.

Around my neck was a set of rosary beads, which had been sent to me by a friend. I knew the Muslim would not appreciate the significance of a Christian symbol, but I offered it to him nonetheless, explaining that it was simply a symbol of my goodwill towards him and therefore not in violation of his religion. I told him to hold on to the rosary and I would in turn think of him. He accepted the gesture gratefully, then lapsed again into his delirium.

The doctor began to administer the Maha Chai version of antibiotics – tetracycline. As I understood it, tetracycline was a leftover from the Second World War; a cheap, almost poisonous drug which was no longer used in any progressive society. It was administered to us as a treatment for almost any ailment. When treating a cut or a wound, the doctor would simply break a cap of tetracycline in two and sprinkle the powder on the wound, which then seemed to heal quickly. Still, it seemed a dubious, old-fashioned remedy.

The Muslim was moved to Lard Yao, a hospital prison attached to the notorious Bang Kwang. As far as I was concerned, the man would probably be going there to die.

Some nine months later, however, I saw the Muslim again. He was running down the corridor, shouting to me. As he approached, he threw his arms around my neck and began hugging me and kissing me on the cheek. I was amazed to see that he was still alive, let alone that he had the ability to run. He showed me his foot and there was nothing but a tiny scar. He was so grateful, constantly thanking me for my best wishes. He handed the rosary back to me, saying that without it and my thoughts for him he would have surely died.

For the first time in my life, I began to wonder seriously about God. My life being the way it was, it seemed to make perfect sense to do that.

* * *

I was eventually released from the darkroom, after three months. I suppose they thought it best that I acclimatise, and so I was placed in one of the hotrooms in Building Nine. Best not throw me back out into the land of the living too quickly.

I'd been here before, so I knew what to expect: the sweating walls, the red ants, the mosquitoes, no toilet at all. In many ways, the hotrooms were worse than the darkrooms, the only difference being that I did have some semblance of privacy, and I was never inside for more than a week. But there was something about the hotrooms that was to make me fear them terribly.

After two days, I was awoken one night to hear the distinct sound of a woman's voice. I couldn't tell where it was coming from – it appeared neither near nor far away, just there – and it seemed to echo eerily throughout the building. I resigned myself to the fact that I was finally going mad and, comfortable enough with that idea, went back to sleep.

The following day, I mentioned this voice to the Thai prisoner in the cell next to mine, expecting him to laugh and agree that I was nuts. To my surprise, he had heard the voice too. He also claimed to know who it came from. Building Nine, he said, used to be the women's prison, a place of terrible reputation where rape and murder were daily occurrences. He believed the voice belonged to the spirit of a woman who had died in the prison, and this was a belief shared by many of the other prisoners and guards as well. Then he told me that he had seen the woman for himself.

One night in the hotroom, he said, he was awakened by a sense that somebody was in the room with him. In a half-sleep, he turned on his mat and immediately felt that there was a figure lying next to him. When he opened his eyes to see, there was nothing there, so he rolled over and went to sleep. He had only just drifted off again when he felt a forceful push in the back which sent him rolling off the mat and onto the floor. As he turned to see what had done this, he saw it. Although the room was dark, he could see the figure on the mat was that of a woman. Her body was beautiful and she had long, wavy hair. He couldn't see her face as she was facing in the other direction, but he somehow knew she would be beautiful. As he approached her, however, she seemed to simply dissolve into the blackness of the room, leaving him wondering whether he had dreamed the whole incident.

Not long afterwards, he had his answer. Very early one morning, when it was still dark, he awoke to an awful commotion in the common section of Building Nine. A prisoner had been found hanging from a water pipe, barely alive but still conscious. Suicides were common in Maha Chai, but this one was baffling for the fact that this particular prisoner had been due for release in only a few days. When questioned as to why he had done this, the prisoner seemed vague, repeating over and over something about a woman with a beautiful voice.

Much later, when he had come to his senses, the prisoner told how he had risen in the middle of the night to find the door of his cell opened. As he emerged, he saw the figure of a woman facing away from him and gliding slowly down the corridor, whispering a tune that compelled him to follow. Upon reaching the common toilet block, the woman stopped and began to turn, whereupon she showed her face for the first time. The prisoner could not remember exactly what he saw, but said it was so terrible it nearly made him faint. The face told him to come with her, and that was the last he remembered.

* * *

When I was released from the hotroom, I was so dehydrated my tongue had swelled up in my mouth, making it nearly impossible to speak. I was taken to the hospital, where I begged the doctor for water, only to be told that water was the worst thing in the world I could have at that time. I was placed on a glucose drip and, after a few days, the doctor began to dab a few drops of water on my tongue every few hours.

As I lay on the hospital bed, drifting in and out of consciousness, I kept promising myself that I would be a good prisoner from now on. I had come to Bangkok as a man doubtful of any superstitious tale, but I was deeply fearful of Building Nine and I never wanted to be there again.

* * *

One morning, Paul received some shocking news. His brother, Gary, had been killed in a freak car accident. Paul was naturally devastated. I did my best to console him, but knew there was little I could do or say to ease his pain. Paul and I had always felt something of a bond, apart from everything else, through the fact that we both had brothers called Gary, and I knew that if it were my brother and not his that had died, while I was locked in this place, I'd most likely go mad with grief.

Over the next couple of days, I couldn't help thinking of my own brother and how little I knew of him. We were separated by nine years, so we had led very different lives while growing up. He was supportive and protective of me, as most older brothers are, but it seemed sad to me that we had never come to know each other better.

I recalled one moment where he had almost betrayed a deep sensitivity. We were watching the film *Spartacus*, of all things, and, while both mature enough to know that it was just an overblown gladiator epic, there was something about it that struck a chord. Right at the end of the film, Spartacus is crucified by the side of the road, moments away from death, convinced that his wife and their new-born child have been returned to a life of slavery. Suddenly, his family appear on the road before him, being smuggled from the country in a horse-drawn cart. The woman jumps from the cart and stands at the feet of her dying husband, holding their child up for him to see.

'Look, Spartacus,' she cries. 'Your son is free.'

As the film ended, I turned to look at my brother and saw that he had been crying.

Now, I wondered about that. Freedom had not been an issue in our lives back then. It certainly was today. I wondered how Gary felt about his little brother being held captive someplace. I wanted to break free from the walls of Maha Chai and make up for the time we'd already lost.

It was only a few days after Paul's news that The Old Man approached me with a sombre look on his face. There was a telegram in his hand. For me.

The message told of how there had been a mistake. It was not Paul's brother Gary who had died in a car accident, but mine.

I ran. I ran through the corridors and out into the yard. I ran at top speed. I kept running until I came to a wall, then turned and ran the other way. Something had just punched the heart right out of my chest and I was completely hysterical. I couldn't stay still and stand in this terrible life. I wanted to run so fast that this world I was living in would cease to exist, that everything around me would stop being real and become nothing but a blur that didn't have me in it. I came to the wall at the hospital and I turned and ran again, faster and faster. The guards were chasing me but I couldn't see for tears and I didn't care where I was going. Whenever I slowed, I felt the reality of this news coming closer and I'd start to run again. I just wanted to break through the walls and keep running until every miserable fucking skerrick of my life had been left far behind, way out of reach of my memory. I wanted to die.

I came to a stop in Building One and collapsed on the floor in a sobbing heap. The guards picked me up in preparation for a beating. Then someone appeared and said something about a bit of bad news.

Days later, still in shock, I received a letter from my brother telling me that he was coming to visit me soon. It was dated a few days before he had died, which was 11 October 1980. I remember the date very well. It was two years to the day since I was arrested in Bangkok.

In those two years, I had experienced all kinds of pain and fear, but none of it was as crushing as that day when I heard my brother was dead. I felt so utterly helpless – unable to perform the simplest show of love by attending his funeral with my family.

I miss my brother so terribly, even now. I can scarcely say any more about this.

* * *

On Saturday nights in Building Three, prisoners with good ratings were allowed upstairs to a room where the guards had a television set. Thai television was not the most dazzling entertainment in the world, but it was better than watching the bugs. We'd gather around and sit in silence as a programme many of us didn't understand flickered about in front of us like a magic thing from the future.

On this particular evening, there was a new guard in Building Three, as the regular guard had become drowsy and was taking a nap. Capitalising on the new guard's ignorance, several prisoners from other buildings crept in to the television room and watched too. The room became crowded, and took on the feeling of some kind of wartime cinema for GIs.

Suddenly, the regular guard appeared, still out of uniform and wearing nothing but a sarong. Seeing the unwelcomed guests, he promptly ordered that the gates to Building Three be locked so that nobody could escape. He then ordered everyone downstairs and told us all to squat on the floor. He told the junior guard to fetch his bamboo cane.

The guard walked slowly around and, as he recognised those of us who belonged in Building Three, tapped us on the shoulder with his cane and told us we were free to leave. He then began asking the others why they were here and who had given them permission to enter the building. Very few answers were satisfactory.

Eventually, he came to an 18-year-old Thai prisoner who was

fairly new to Building Three. The Thai boy answered all the questions that were asked of him, and in time the guard told him to stand and leave. With this, the boy stood and bowed to the guard, a gesture he no doubt believed to be one of respect or thanks. Out of nowhere, the guard struck him viciously across the face with his cane. The boy seemed to be completely stung by the shock of it. He reacted out of pure mechanical outrage. He began throwing wild punches at the guard, with some of them connecting heavily. One struck the guard so hard that he fell to the floor, and for a moment it looked as if Maha Chai was about to have a mutiny on its hands. But the room was full of guards and blueboys now, who quickly restrained the Thai boy until he was still.

The beaten guard stood to his feet and ordered the guards to take the prisoner to a room at the end of the building.

Whatever any of us did for the next hour in Building Three was accompanied by the sound of the young Thai boy being beaten mercilessly. He was then taken to Building Two.

For three months we didn't see him. I presumed we'd never see him again, but we did. He was a walking skeleton. His skin was as grey as that of an elephant and peeling so badly it looked as if he'd been soaked in hot water for days before being rubbed with sandpaper. He was hunched over in a squatting position as he walked, and his eyes were puffed out so that they seemed only to be slits in fat flesh. Apparently, they had placed him in a tiny wooden cage, only big enough for a man who rolled himself into a ball. They had then suspended the box from a hook and chain in the ceiling. A sarong was placed over the cage, so that even the false light that came from the dark spaces of the room could not penetrate his world. There he had stayed for the three months, to think about his temper.

The guard who he had struck had time to think about his own temper too, but he had come to no new conclusions after three months. Upon releasing the Thai boy, the first thing he had the guards do was drag him out into the yard and hold his face to the blinding afternoon sun.

They might just as well have left the Thai boy in the cage forever. He was only with us again for the briefest of time. I don't know what happened to him after this. He was taken away a few days later and we never saw him again. Nobody asked after him. There wasn't any point in knowing.

* * *

Two Thais were thrown into a cell with seven other Thai prisoners, who were murderous. In an orgy of violence one evening, the Thais fiercely raped the newcomers until their bodies were limp with confusion and pain. The guards frowned upon rape in Maha Chai, and the following day the Thais were punished. They were marched through the centre of the building, where the rest of us were encouraged to hurl abuse and throw anything we could. They were then taken to the yard and executed.

But what was the point? The damage had been done. It had been allowed to be done. Nobody cared that these men were executed. We cared that the other prisoners had been brutalised and their minds reduced to wreckage. Yet we were invited – no, forced, actually – to take part in the hollow punishment. We were simply part of the barbarism of Maha Chai. We had been in Maha Chai for nearly three years. The waiting for our trial to end had been horribly long.

Oh, fuck, I hated this place. So much that it made me wish the entire human race would become extinct.

CHAPTER **8**

TRIAL

Capt Vyraj Jutimitta,
Narc Suppression Unit,
Bangkok

4 October 1978

Dear Vyraj,

YESTERDAY, THE 3RD OCTOBER, 1978, I received a cable from
Canberra, stating that a WARREN FELLOWS, using a false
passport in the name of GREGORY HASTINGS BARKER and in
the company of a PAUL CECIL HAYWARD, had boarded a flight
two days ago bound for Thailand, presumably Bangkok.
FELLOWS, alias BARKER, was allowed to leave Australia, despite
being recognised, in the hope that he might return to Bangkok so
that you could detain him for his attempt to smuggle heroin from
Bangkok to Australia in February this year.

Further information suggested that both FELLOWS, alias
BARKER, and HAYWARD intend to smuggle heroin to Australia in
specially designed and prepared suitcases, which makes detection of

the heroin almost impossible. Special inserts have been prepared to be removed by screws and then rescrewed and set with a quick drying resin, once the heroin is in place.

Yesterday evening I met an informant who told me that he had met two men in the company of other suspects known to me, and described the man BARKER, whom he had met before, but could not remember his name. I showed him a photograph of FELLOWS, and he then confirmed that both BARKER and HAYWARD were in Bangkok. I asked the informant to contact the two suspects today in Patpong, which he did. He again confirmed that they are BARKER and HAYWARD. He told me that they had an appointment at lunchtime at the MONTEIN HOTEL to meet 'a man'. The informant then arranged to meet them between 3 p.m. and 5 p.m. today, at the Bangkok Sports Club to play snooker.

I contacted a friend at Qantas and have ascertained that both suspects booked a return flight to Sydney on QF6 on Wednesday the 11th October. The friend will contact me if they should change the bookings. I then contacted a friend, known to you, at the Montein Hotel, and have confirmed that the suspects occupy rooms 413 and 415. I intend to visit the Montein later today and receive copies of their registration card, and request details of any phone calls, etc. I believe that the meeting today was to arrange delivery of the narcotics, suspected to be heroin or cocaine.

Since arriving in Bangkok, these two suspects have been in the company of a number of known and suspected traffickers, persons involved in gambling, racing and organised crime in Australia, including associates who are wanted on warrants of arrest in Australia and Thailand, and who, when arrested, will be deported as undesirable aliens. I have so far organised, through Col. Bamroong and General Saneh, and General Anant of Immigration, warrants of arrest for two convicted traffickers, known to have business in Patpong and Pattaya, and whom I suspect of organising the exportation of 600 kilos of Thai sticks concealed in safes, to

Australia recently and which is the subject of current enquiries with BMNU and myself. These two traffickers apparently are aware of the warrants, and have been leaving Thailand and returning through Singapore and Malaysia to avoid detection. I can supply you with background information if you so desire, on these and others, in whom I have an interest.

A discreet surveillance of BARKER and HAYWARD may lead to a supplier, who, if identified, can be arrested after BARKER and HAYWARD depart for the airport. We are not seeking to let the heroin run to Australia, as it would assist you to arrest them at DON MUANG, and possibly clear up the other exportation case by FELLOWS, alias BARKER, earlier this year . . .

* * *

For years I had wondered about our arrest, and the events that preceded it. How long had we been under surveillance? Were we set up? Was there any time when we could have changed our minds and slipped away from this web, or were we destined for these Thai prisons before we even left our homes? Over the three years that spanned our trial, I watched the little mysteries of my life unfold.

* * *

Mad Dog had been on my tail since February 1978. In his evidence, he claimed to have received a telephone call in that month from the United Transportation Company, a shipping firm located at a dockyard in Bangkok. A man named Warren Fellows, an Australian, had booked and paid for transportation of a parcel. When asked for his passport, however, he appeared to panic, made some excuse and left, never to return. When he had not returned one month later, the company became suspicious and called the police.

Mad Dog went to the scene and discovered that the parcel did indeed contain drugs. He then mobilised the Bangkok Drug Suppression Unit to search for Warren Fellows. At that time, I was already in Australia.

Nevertheless, I was gone from that moment. Had I never returned to Bangkok, you would not be reading this story.

Mad Dog liaised with Australian Federal Police in Bangkok, who then raised the alarm in Sydney. I was then under watch constantly.

After receiving a cable from Canberra stating that Paul and myself were on our way to Thailand, Australian police in Bangkok let Mad Dog know we were on our way.

His report said he had sent his men out to conduct surveillance and had learned of our plans to leave Bangkok on a Qantas flight on 11 October at 3.00 p.m. He arranged for us to be searched before we set off for the airport, in case we slipped through. During his surveillance, he and his officials watched me and Paul bump into The Old Man at Natty Gems, and watched us fighting at the Texan Bar.

Mad Dog's testimony then turned into a fable. He claimed that he had seen us meet many times with The Old Man, in all sorts of bars and restaurants all over Bangkok. This was just part of his desperation to get The Old Man, who he obviously wanted to put in jail more than he did myself and Paul.

He also claimed that 'Fellows admitted directly and bluntly that the heroin was not in his room but had been taken to Hayward's room for keeping.'

I have never understood why this lie was necessary.

There was also the matter of the mystery phone call that was made to my room at the Montein Hotel while police officers were making their search.

Mad Dog claimed he answered the call himself. The caller, he claimed, spoke English with an Australian accent and had a hoarse voice. He asked for Mr Barker. Told he wasn't there, the caller asked who was speaking. Mad Dog claimed he said he was the cleaner and the caller hung up.

'Who was that?' he allegedly asked me.

'Why, The Old Man,' I allegedly answered. 'We had an appointment to meet at Natty Gems at 9.30.'

'Why did you have to go to see Mr Sinclair?'

'We had to see him before taking the suitcase to the airport to smuggle the heroin.'

Then, claimed Mad Dog, there was another phone call to the room, whereupon he did the same thing as before by picking up the phone and saying he was the cleaner.

What detective in his right mind would do that not once, but twice? Wouldn't a well-drilled policeman – any policeman – order me to pick up the phone then snatch it from me once I had said a few words? This was rubbish, once again designed to put The Old Man in jail.

I'm not trying to suggest that I was wrongly convicted by corrupt police officers. Simply that I was rightfully convicted by corrupt police officers.

At one point in the trial, Mad Dog actually tried to harass the judge by picking up the witness stand and moving it closer to his table. The judge warned Mad Dog that if he continued this behaviour he would send him from the court.

Shortly after this warning was given, this judge was replaced with another. Judge Travorn.

* * *

For a couple of years we had been going to court every few weeks, so when it came to the day of our sentencing I was tense, but somewhat relieved. I'd hated the ritual with the chats, the old bus through the city, the heavily armed guards, the M16s, the stopping of the traffic as we were paraded out.

As I have said, the court was a farce to begin with. Judge Travorn seemed to have made his mind up before he even saw us.

Some days, if I'd had no heroin, I'd be sick as we went, the peculiarity of motion being too much to bear.

I was glad for this chapter to end.

There was no doubt that Paul and I had been caught with the heroin – that was plain. What I was hoping for was that Travorn would believe there to be enough evidence suggesting that Paul was something of an unwitting accomplice. I also believed that The Old Man would probably get off lightly, but this may have been a product of my certainty of his innocence in this particular affair. For myself, I expected the worst.

By now, I understood quite a bit of the Thai language, so I basically knew what was being said. My lawyer translated the rest.

After reviewing the facts brought before him, Judge Travorn was of the opinion that the actions of myself, Paul Hayward, The Old Man and Noi were obviously those of a group who wished to possess and distribute narcotics. The verdict was guilty for all.

Travorn then went on to pass sentence. He had taken into account Paul's lesser degree of involvement, along with his apparent distance from the source: The Old Man.

Hearing his name mentioned, though understanding nothing of what was being said, The Old Man began nervously nattering to his lawyer, who seemed to be telling him to be quiet. I realised at this point the fascinating miscarriage that was taking place before us: the Thai judicial system had completely swallowed the evidence stating that I had been working on the orders of The Old Man who, they believed, was the brains behind the operation. This was shocking news for him, but a fortunate mistake for Paul. There had been no evidence to suggest that Paul had ever been acquainted with The Old Man. He might get off lightly after all.

Travorn then announced that Paul Hayward was sentenced to 30 years. Three more decades of this place. My God.

Travorn then declared that myself, The Old Man and Noi would each be sentenced to life imprisonment.

Although I was expecting the worst when I walked into this courtroom, the sound of the word 'life' made my knees buckle and my throat tighten in revolt. My life and everything in it was now gone, replaced by this 'life' – this stinking, hateful, loveless, hopeless 'life'.

The Old Man was now going berserk with frustration, trying to get the attention of his lawyer, who was still holding up his hand and telling him to be quiet. The poor old bastard didn't yet understand that the remainder of his life had just been annihilated. Eventually, he leaned over to me and begged for the news. With a deadpan delivery that was completely unintentional and out of my control, I said to him: 'We got the lot.'

The look on his face was indescribable.

I was free from Maha Chai. That was good.

But I was going to a place that was even more feared. Bang Kwang.

The Thais called it Big Tiger. They said it prowled and ate.

CHAPTER 9

BIG TIGER

THE MAN IN CHARGE of our transfer was an official who knew Paul and me from Maha Chai, where he had been governor for a short time. For some reason, he had taken a liking to us and at one point had actually opened an account for us in the food store, with his own money.

After our sentences were passed down, we were taken aside for processing, whereupon this man informed us of his intention to have us sent to Lard Yao, a much less severe prison than Bang Kwang. He was of the opinion that Bang Kwang was an evil place where no foreigner should be sent, no matter how serious their crime.

* * *

Once inside Lard Yao, we were placed in a cell with about 20 others in Building Five. We were to stay here for one month while the prison officers determined our prisoner ratings, which ranged from 'excellent' to 'poor'. The difficult thing about maintaining a good prison rating was that there was no way to survive for anyone who stayed within the boundaries of the rules. In order to live and stay sane, you quite simply had to break the rules. In this cell, there were practically no prisoners adhering to the rules. All of them that I could see were using drugs, which were plentiful in Lard Yao. Provided you weren't caught, sedating yourself with drugs was the best way to keep a low profile.

The first night in Lard Yao was miserable. Somebody in a cell not far away was murdered and we heard it all. This whole experience had taken on a new meaning at this time. Before, there had been a sense that everything was temporary, that being incarcerated in Thailand was something that would come to an end one day. While the trial was still proceeding, it seemed as if there was hope – a feeble hope, for sure, but any amount of hope was enough to light the way. Now there was the knowledge that this was final and irreversible. This was my life. These dark nights in crowded rooms with the echoes of prisoners sobbing and moaning – this was as good as life was to be from now on.

It's astonishing how you can distract yourself from reality for so much of a day. In the moments when reality really hits you, when it really presents itself clearly and unavoidably, you wonder how you've managed to ignore it for so long. On this night, I couldn't believe that I had been alive in this situation for the time that I had. I wondered why I hadn't died of heartbreak or fear, seeing that those feelings were so constant. This dreadful, crystal-clear realisation drifted into my mind and then seemed to evaporate just as quickly. It was as if the person I once was had just entered my body again and, seeing the situation was so totally awful, had left before it could feel the pain for longer than a second. I closed my eyes and tried to sleep.

One morning, after only five days in Lard Yao, Paul, The Old Man and I were awoken and told that the governor wanted to see us. It was bad news.

The Old Man had apparently tried to bribe a guard for one thing or another and, not having bothered to become familiar enough with the system during all of this time, had chosen his guard badly, trying to bribe an actual building chief. The three of us were still considered partners in this whole affair, as if we were one animal with several brains. The governor considered us a grave security risk in Lard Yao, and said he had no alternative but to send us to Bang Kwang.

I was well aware of Bang Kwang's reputation as quite simply the most feared prison in the world. While doing my business in Bangkok, I had been aware of the possibility that, if caught, I may be sent to Big Tiger. But somehow it had seemed a distant chance – I did not belong in Bang Kwang. It was a place for the lowest, most hopeless forms of humanity. Nobody thinks of themselves in that way. Not even criminals.

Shackled in our chains, we were hustled into the truck for the last time. We were now going to the end point – there was no heavier prison than the one to which we were headed. This was the end of the line.

As we approached the gate, I couldn't believe how enormous Big Tiger looked, looming ahead of us like a monstrosity. I was terrified. For years I had listened to the legend of this place and now I was seeing it, approaching it. It seemed to be drawing me in and humming with hatred, like a massive, living machine of misery.

As if to exaggerate the fact that we were entering a desolate world, the gardens outside the prison were ornate and luxurious, spilling over walls and hedges like some last reminder of the paradise that we were leaving outside. Not only that, but it seemed to tell of a certain extravagance – a sense that, here, the punishment suffered would be lavish and indulgent. The sadism and suffering that boiled in its belly made the Big Tiger rich and gloriously satisfied.

This is a Thai philosophy. The unjust, the sinners, are worthless and to be destroyed. Those who destroy them are righteous and godlike.

I watched all the doors slam behind me. There seemed so many of them it was hard to believe all of them could have served any purpose other than to rob those entering of any hope.

We were then marched down a long road which led to the main prison area. I saw the cages and the bars in the visiting area. The flies were swarming on my face, as if to welcome me to my new home. I could smell the stench of the open sewage and the nearby rubbish tip. There was a building straight ahead with a sign that read, 'Building One: Indoctrination building'. I could scarcely take another step. My legs and my mind were jelly.

After being processed, The Old Man managed to convince the doctors to let him remove his chains. I think they allowed this purely on account of his age. Paul and I were told that we would have to remain in ours for at least a month. This wasn't so surprising. By this point, I almost felt as if the chains were a part of my body.

Before being sent to our new home in Building Two, Paul and I were lectured on the basic principles of Bang Kwang. It was the same as all the other prisons. We were to wake at 6.00 a.m., wash, eat and sit in the yard until late afternoon when we would return to our cells. We were informed of the three methods of punishment: Building Six, which was where you were sent permanently if you were proving to be particularly difficult; solitary confinement, or *khan deo,* in tiny cells not unlike those in Maha Chair and the 'red rooms', two-metres square and desperately uncomfortable, but preferable to the stone-cold isolation of *khan deo.* There were several other forms of punishment in Big Tiger which they did not tell us about during our indoctrination. We would find out soon enough.

* * *

The yard in Bang Kwang seemed smaller than those in the other prisons, but that might have been an illusion created by the mass of prisoners. It was so unbelievably crowded that if you didn't make it to the yard early in the day there was simply nowhere to sit. Not that there was any point in sitting, for there was nothing to do.

Beds were nothing but straw mats and pillows of any kind were not allowed. The prison was hot with fleas, and I contracted lice within days, forcing me to shave my head.

All the water we had at our disposal came from the local river, which was little more than a stream of muddy red filth. We were expected to use this same water for bathing and drinking. This water was pumped from the river via a pipe that was about 50 metres downstream from the prison sewage outlet. We were drinking and bathing in our own waste.

One day, I saw them emptying the water from the troughs, exchanging it for supposedly fresh water. It was obviously a long time since it had been changed, for the bottom of the trough was coated in a thick, brown moss. Another time, I turned on one of the taps and a small fish fell out into my hands. I'd never caught a fish in my life until I went to Bang Kwang.

The common toilets were the same: holes in the floor with no walls or barriers at all. And the food was the usual Thai prison fare: red rice, perhaps a fish skeleton, perhaps a bowl of pig slop. Meat was forbidden. They were starving us to weakness.

Rats, however, ran riot in the prison and there was no way the guards could prevent a prisoner from eating them. One prisoner had actually cultivated a rat farm against the wall of his cell. Every Saturday morning, he'd hold a little market and sell the fattened rats to other prisoners. There were cages with the rats in them, on display, as in a butcher's shop. A few packets of cigarettes was all the buyer required for a side of rat. The butcher would chop the rat into desired portions or, for a little extra, he could create a stew or whatever you preferred. These weren't sewer rats – they were a better quality. A higher gourmet standard, the butcher said. He told me that eating rats was not unusual in the Thai countryside. Thai farmers were known to chase these rats when they saw them in a field, spike them on the end of a stick and roast them over a fire. They were considered a delicacy in some areas.

I believed him. I'd been hungry for years now and was willing to accept any story that would make me able to eat that which I normally couldn't stomach.

* * *

We had only been in Big Tiger for a few days when Paul was faced with a showdown. He was approached in the visiting area by a Black American prisoner who seemed to have a problem with the way Paul was looking at him. Paul had been staring at the man, but only because he was marvelling at his size. This man was enormous and Paul, at that time, only weighed about 70 kilos. As Paul looked at the man, he turned and told Paul to mind his own business.

'Get out of my face, man,' he shouted. 'Do you want to break concrete or what?'

The other prisoners heard this and turned to see what Paul would do. Paul realised immediately that whatever happened at this moment could affect the rest of his time in Big Tiger. If he backed down, he might find himself being abused and walked over by anyone in the prison.

'No,' he said to the American, 'I don't want to break concrete. But I'll be happy to put your head through that cage over there.' The American wasn't surprised at this retort. It appeared that he knew something about Paul's history.

'All right, man,' he leered. 'I know you used to be a boxer, so let's see what you can do.'

The American leaned over Paul, challenging him to take a shot. He looked utterly indestructible, and Paul seemed to momentarily be questioning his own wisdom. The American seized the moment, before Paul could even put up his guard, and sent a punch crashing into his jaw. The sound of the punch was sickening, and Paul hauled the American towards him, holding himself upright as his knees buckled from beneath him. For a moment it looked as if Paul was never going to be able to get his legs working again. But this was only temporary.

As if hit by some kind of electric jolt, Paul threw himself back, stood upright and charged, laying several fast punches into the huge body in front of him, before landing a thumping left hand into the American's head. The surprised American fell to the ground, but quickly got back to his feet. Completely enraged, he lunged at Paul, who again landed several shattering punches to his head and body. Once again, the American toppled under the weight of Paul's fury, only this time he was not so quick to stand. When he finally did, he began moving away from Paul, muttering something about how he was going to get his revenge on Paul later. As far as the American was concerned, the fight was over.

But in Paul's mind, the result was only half-achieved. He wanted the prisoners of Bang Kwang to know that if they were going to take him on, they were not going to be able to do so and walk away murmuring continual insults. He moved swiftly towards the American, smashing his fist into his face. Blood spurted from the American's eye as he tumbled to the floor for a third time.

At this moment, the American's friends moved between him and Paul, declaring that Paul had made his point. The American continued with now-garbled insults, but was hauled away by his friends. The only injury Paul sustained was a cut on his middle finger.

From that moment forward, Paul had the respect of the other prisoners. Even the Black American approached Paul the following day to apologise, and they later became friends. This sort of grudging respect was common in Bang Kwang.

Sometime after the event, however, Paul confided in me that he was fighting that day out of sheer terror. I remember very clearly what he said.

'I've played football with some of the biggest, hardest men you could possibly come up against in Australian first-grade football, and my whole body has been hit fucking hard. I've boxed and been hit, too. But never in my whole life have I been hit like I was that day. When that guy gave me his biggest punch, the only thing that kept me on my feet was that my heart was pumping. That's the hardest I've ever, ever, ever, ever been hit. My legs were gone and I don't know how I stayed up. I honestly don't know how I stayed on my feet.'

I remember feeling lucky to be friends in here with a man who wasn't prepared to go down for anything.

* * *

The authorities in Big Tiger did not appear to be quite as lenient with regard to drugs. All visitors were heavily searched, and those of suspect nature were practically turned inside out, so getting the drugs into the prison was a difficult business. But, as usual, the Thais had found many ways around this problem.

One method was to place the heroin inside a small tin, usually one that had contained Tiger Balm. The heroin would be packed inside and the whole tin then swallowed by a Thai who was careful not to let the tin enter his stomach. I don't know quite how they did it, but somehow they managed to keep the tin wedged in their throats. Once inside the prison, the Thai would regurgitate the tin.

Some guards were aware of this procedure and would do their best to extract the drugs from the courier. One time, a guard conducted a thorough search of a Thai's mouth with his flashlight. On another occasion, a guard was so convinced that the visiting Thai had heroin in his throat that he sat him down and forced him to eat rice and drink water. The Thai kept arguing that he was not hungry, but the guard insisted, watching closely as the Thai unenthusiastically munched on the rice. Suddenly, as the Thai was trying to swallow, the guard lunged forward and grabbed him by the neck, forcing the tins of heroin up and out of the Thai's mouth.

'Good boy, good boy,' smiled the guard.

He then delivered the Thai a brutal thrashing.

On this same day, the head of security, a man called Sucha, called me over to help him. A foreign prisoner had just been visited by a representative from his embassy, and Sucha wanted me to translate a message to this prisoner. Apparently, the prisoner had complained bitterly to the embassy official, who had in turn made comments of a threatening nature towards the prison staff, vowing to ensure that the prisoner's complaints would be investigated.

Sucha stared the prisoner in the eye as I translated his words.

'Your embassy comes once a month, and you get 30 minutes with them. Get this perfectly clear – the other 30 days, I've got you for every minute. Do you understand?'

* * *

I hadn't been in Bang Kwang long before I saw the ultimate torture. It was a blend of physical and mental breakdown and it was typical of the methods used by the guards in Bang Kwang to break the spirit of the inmates.

A Thai prisoner was led out of his cell and into the yard. He was naked but for a blindfold. His hands were brought behind him and tied. He was then made to kneel, as if in prayer.

Slowly, three guards with canes began to walk around the prisoner. Their steps were slow and deliberate, and they made sure that the sound of their boots gently crushing the dirt beneath them was loud enough for the prisoner to have to concentrate on. After circling the prisoner in this fashion for several minutes, the guards stopped. Then one of the guards tapped him lightly on the face with his cane. The prisoner blanched as he awaited what he thought would be a strike to the face. Several seconds passed with nothing, then the cane came crashing down onto the prisoner's back, making him scream in pain and shock.

Again, the guards began their slow, methodical march around the prisoner, stopping once again after a few minutes. Just as before, the cane would tap the prisoner gently on the face. The prisoner squeezed his shoulder-blades together, convinced that he was about to feel the crack of the cane on his back. A few moments passed, then one of the other guards brought his cane smacking into the prisoner's face. The guards waited until the tormented prisoner had recovered from the shock, then their march began again.

After nearly an hour of this, the prisoner was an emotional wreck. His mind had been assaulted in so many ways as it attacked itself with questions. When would the marching stop? How long after it stopped would the tap from the cane come? Which part of the body would the cane touch and what did that mean? After each strike, would the march begin again or had the guards had enough of this game?

Physical pain is hard enough to bear, but when coupled with this sort of torture it is appalling. In the end, the prisoner seemed not to even feel the physical anguish. His face was distorted purely from the mental torture of it all.

In Bang Kwang, the guards were encouraged to brainwash the prisoners into creatures who could no longer function mentally. They worked on the body and, when that no longer had the desired effect, they attacked the mind. And they were experts at destroying human will.

Not long after witnessing this barbarism for the first time, I saw another Thai tortured in a similar fashion. I'm not sure what he'd done to deserve it – probably very little – but the guards had him tied to a pole and were beating him with the canes. They began in the usual fashion but, instead of continuing with the slow frequency of the beating, they seemed to slowly work their way into a fury. They beat him so badly I could not understand why he was still alive and breathing. His skin was broken and streaming with blood. A bone on his arm was sticking out through the flesh and his legs were crippled and misshapen. I thought for sure that the guards would beat him until he was dead. As if sensing they had pushed him to within an inch of his life, the guards stopped. But rather than drag him back to his cell, or to the hospital where he truly belonged, the head guard took a stick of incense, set it alight and placed it in the prisoner's broken and bloodied hand.

In the distance, at the end of the yard, was a statue of Buddha which was used by some of the Thais and Chinese for worship. The guard ordered the beaten prisoner to crawl to the statue on his hands and knees and pray for forgiveness. The prisoner could barely open his eyes to look for the direction of the statue, let alone crawl to it, but the guard was firm. The prisoner, he said, must do this to rid himself of the shame and the dishonour he had brought upon himself. Without the forgiveness and mercy of Buddha, the prisoner deserved to die.

As mangled as he was, the man somehow managed to lift his stomach from the dirt. He began dragging his body, one inch at a time, with the incense stick still burning in his hand. It took him forever to cover several metres, but he crawled on, his blood smearing the earth behind him.

By the time he reached Buddha, the incense was nearly burned away. In a state of near collapse, he bowed his head at the feet of the statue. He clung to it as if it were his mother. He bowed his head to the dirt and prayed as the guards watched with a mixture of satisfaction and disgust.

I wondered what he prayed to Buddha about, and how, if Buddha was indeed the man's god, he had been able to sit on his spiritual throne and watch such a scene.

CHAPTER 10

DEATH

THERE WAS ONLY ONE person known to have ever escaped from Bang Kwang. He was a Thai national who had seven charges against him and had been sentenced to death for three of them. His execution was imminent. On the evening of his escape, he had been sent to a punishment cell on the fourth floor of Building Six. He was heavily chained and was in the cell completely alone.

At sometime during the night, he had managed to slip out of his chains. Nobody knew exactly how he did this, but there were those who had seen him perform this trick before, using a sarong. This was a miraculous feat in itself, but he then managed to somehow escape from his cell, probably by bribing a guard. The next morning, guards found a gash in the mesh which enclosed the building, obviously cut with some sharp implement. On the little stretch of grass that separated the building from the outer wall of Big Tiger, they found three sarongs tied together and all attached to a makeshift grappling hook. The Thai had scaled the walls and slipped out into the night.

Not one of the guards had seen or heard a thing. Nor, it appeared, had any of the prisoners. The guards questioned the man in the cell next door, convinced that he must have seen or heard something. The man, who was somewhat backward, would only say one word: *chima,* which means 'the ghost come'. Being deeply superstitious, the guards chose to leave the man alone and drop the matter completely.

There was a belief among the Thais that when a prisoner died, his ghost returned briefly to his cell. Sometimes, on the night after a prisoner's death, the Thais would leave food or cigarettes for the man who had passed away, and there were many stories told of cigarettes that smouldered during the night, or food that had disappeared by morning. These incidents can, of course, be easily explained in a prison where cigarettes and food are such sought-after properties, but there were some tales that were convincing nonetheless. A clash with guards could often be avoided by playing on their beliefs in such things.

Apart from this one Thai prisoner, however, there was no person known who had ever escaped from Big Tiger without dying first. Death, it seemed, was the only sure way to freedom.

Every few months, somebody was executed in Big Tiger. News of a pending execution was broadcast a few hours prior to the event, and all prisoners would be ordered to their cells. These were miserable times. A darkness would fall over the whole prison and nobody spoke. There was death and sadness all around us in Bang Kwang, but it usually occurred suddenly and without fanfare. When we knew it was coming, deliberate and intentional, it was as if we could feel the spirit of death travelling across the land towards us. We could hear it enter the buildings. We could smell it.

Sometimes, if the guards were in the mood, they would force prisoners to watch these executions. They needn't have bothered, really. Whether we could see the action or not, every one of us could hear and feel it.

These executions would sometimes involve several prisoners being put to death at the same time. But much harder to bear were the times when there was just one. It was so lonely. The prisoner would walk out with his head bowed, seeing his last few minutes before him, alone with nobody but the very people who wished for his death. It was strange how most of them would go so quietly, walking along with their heads bowed to the earth. Perhaps they would cry, but few made a scene. Obeying orders had become second nature, even when the order meant the loss of everything you had.

One time, a Thai prisoner was to be executed alone. For days he had known it was coming, and seemed prepared – as prepared as anyone could be for the ending of their life. He had been praying and silently going about his business, seemingly careful to make his last days as serene and uneventful as possible.

Eventually the time came for him to go. The guards came to his cell and at first he seemed to be going with dignity, resigned to his fate. Suddenly, as the guards led him down the corridor, he began to struggle. His movements weren't violent or forceful, just desperate. He reached out and clung to the wire, sobbing like a child. He didn't make much noise at all, but simply held on, his arms trembling, his eyes filled with a terribly sad determination. A guard began lashing his hands with his cane, but the man wouldn't let go, clinging with all his strength to the last dreadful piece of his life. It was awful to watch him – such a lonely vision. Here was a man who was moving towards his last moments of life and he didn't want to go. He had to know that there was nothing for him in an extra few seconds, or a minute, or even a day. Nothing but more of this horrible, hopeless life in Bang Kwang.

But still he held on. That last sweet minute was everything. And it was spent with tears running from his eyes and a small crowd of men, who had nothing to do with his precious life, brutalising him with sticks.

To go to your death with nobody to whisper even so much as a caring word is the saddest thing I can possibly imagine, and I wish I'd never had to witness such a thing.

* * *

In Big Tiger there were certain prisoners who, through good behaviour, had achieved a privileged status. Known as trusties or 'Blueboys', these prisoners were often murderers or men guilty of crimes of violence, who had simply been cunning enough to secure themselves a decent place in the eyes of the prison system. They wore blue, officer-like uniforms and carried batons. They were still regarded as prisoners, but were trusted by the officials. If a guard wanted to have a sleep during his shift, he might ask a Blueboy to keep an eye on things. Most of them seemed content with the fact that they were now privileged prisoners and treated the others fairly, but others, of course, took the privilege to mean they could now behave as the guards. The Blueboy, having transcended the status of miserable prisoner, was all too often carried away with his freedom.

There was one Blueboy who relentlessly sought favour in the eyes of the prison authorities by informing the guards of nearly everything he saw. Most guards could be coerced into turning a blind eye to dice games or even drugs, but this Blueboy was determined to be the most strict guard in the prison. It didn't seem to occur to him that, in the eyes of the prisoners, he had become the most hated of all staff in Big Tiger.

One morning, after yet another bout of persecution at the hands of this Blueboy, the Thais and Chinese began taking up a collection. There was a Thai prisoner who was to be released that afternoon, and it was said he was leaving the prison with no money and no family on the outside. The prisoners had decided to make him an offer: for 300 baht – the equivalent of about $100 – he was to assault the particular Blueboy before he was released. The Thai could not resist that amount of money, which was probably more than he had ever seen in his life, so he agreed, despite the possibility that his release would almost certainly be stopped.

At around midday, the Thai prisoner went to the toilet with a sheet of newspaper supplied to him by a guard. He emerged sometime later, the newspaper filled with the contents of his bowels. Excited by the prospect of his release, and no doubt nervous about the task we was going to perform, the Thai had been suffering from a mild bout of diarrhoea and had no trouble making sure his little package was as disgusting as it could possibly be.

As the other prisoners watched, he marched up to the office that was being manned by the troublesome Blueboy and knocked on the door. The Blueboy looked irritated as he stood from his chair and approached the prisoner, asking him why he was here. The Thai didn't answer, but simply brought the newspaper and its contents down hard upon the Blueboy's head. It was disgusting.

In their culture, the worst insult you can give to a Thai is to touch him on the head. Many times, I saw foreign prisoners playfully pat a Thai on the head, causing him to go absolutely berserk. Thais believe that a man's head is closest to Buddha, and therefore the highest spiritual point of his body. A man's feet are the lowest – they touch the dirt and the filth of earth – but the head is sacred and personal. Definitely not the place for another man's bag of shit.

This episode is peculiar to Big Tiger in that the expected punishment seemed to happen in reverse. The Thai who committed the insulting act was released that afternoon with seemingly no action taken against him. The Blueboy, on the other hand, was immediately transferred to another building and two weeks later, in an apparently separate incident, he was stabbed by another prisoner. It was as if the guards condoned what had occurred, or at least were prepared to tolerate it. Perhaps they had been smart enough to spot a true creep when they saw one.

* * *

Many of the guards were good to the prisoners, under the circumstances. The ones who dealt heroin were generally respected, for they could get us through the day. But, basically speaking, the guards could not be trusted to come too close.

There was one guard, with whom I had always been quite friendly, who seemed to change his opinion overnight, for no reason that I could see. On this particular day he approached me just before wash time and asked me how I was. Before I could even so much as reply, the guard slapped me hard in the face. Reeling from the blow, I glanced up at him and saw that he was smiling. I asked him what was going on, but he said nothing, his face wearing something like a hateful smile. I then told him if he ever did such a thing again I'd knock him down, to which he did nothing more than laugh and walk away. I was frightened by this, as it seemed to be some sort of prelude to something else.

Less than a week after this event, I noticed that this particular guard had been absent for a few days. After making inquiries, I was told that two days after his altercation with me, the guard had been at home having dinner when there was a knock at the door. His wife answered to a stranger who asked for her husband by name. When the guard came to the door, he was shot in the neck at point-blank range. We would not be seeing him in Big Tiger again. Although he survived the shooting with his life, the bullet had severed his spinal column and he was to live the rest of his life in a wheelchair.

As I have said, it was not wise for guards to get too close to the prisoners. Nor, for that matter, would a guard serve himself by being notoriously cruel.

One day, a guard called Chom entered the exercise yard, which was ridiculously small and almost impossible to perform any exercise in. He spotted a Thai prisoner who was not bothering to exercise and proceeded to beat him. To the astonishment of all who watched, the guard did not stop beating until the prisoner was dead. This incident alone would not have caused too much of a stir, but a few days later the incident was repeated in almost exactly the same fashion, with another Thai being beaten to death by the same guard. The Thai prisoners took up a collection.

A few days later, Chom was leaving the prison after completion of his shift when a shot rang out. The assassins missed, but only just. Chom scurried back into the prison minus an ear.

Thais would tolerate a guard if they had to, but they could get to him if they wanted. Some of the Thais were actually in Bang Kwang by choice. For the well-connected ones, life in here was more stable than the life they might be living in the Thai slums. They had friends, they were part of a team. They were the tough, heartless Thais who liked the chaos and violence. For foreigners, these prisoners were to be respected, but avoided at all costs.

* * *

After two years in Bang Kwang, The Old Man was released. He had appealed against his original sentence and the court had found that there were indeed discrepancies in the evidence that had been used against him. Good luck for The Old Man. I couldn't begrudge anyone the blessing of being released from Big Tiger.

On the day I received the news that my father had passed away, I had been having what could be called a 'good day'. It was 15 February 1984. Nothing had happened, nobody had been hurt yet. Then came the telegram.

I remembered that last visit I had from him in Maha Chai, and only realised then that he had known this was going to happen. For any man who loses his father, it's hard to put the feelings into words. There's a sense that you've lost part of your strength – the very thing he gave to you with his own flesh and blood. For me there was naturally a feeling of being cheated. I had been robbed of something that would only occur once. I hadn't been there for the last years of my father's life. I hadn't been allowed to tell him that I loved him. Somebody hadn't allowed me to do that with my father. It was the same with my brother, although his death was so sudden that nobody had the chance to say goodbye. With Dad, he just disappeared off the face of the planet and I couldn't even see the space that he had left behind. I felt woefully sad for my mother, who was now truly alone.

I cried that day, as I had on the day of Gary's death, but the sadness was different. It was more of a dull, sickened ache than a feeling of tortured despair. The loss was beginning to pile up to the heavens and I was sick of grief. Suddenly, my punishment seemed way out of proportion and I couldn't see the lesson that was to be learned. How much suffering was I to go through before the world agreed that I'd paid my price?

I suppose, in a way, I lost my mind at this point. I began to hit the drugs with a fury. I had almost given up hope completely. I just could not cope with the memory of what my life had been and what it had now become. I'd had so many chances to avoid this fate and I had let them all slip away. Before I had ever been to Bangkok or India, my family had sent me to France, where I was to learn about horses with my cousin. It hadn't worked out and I returned to Australia after less than a year. I had obtained an apprenticeship as a hairdresser in Double Bay, but had decided that wasn't working and gave it away. Could I not have stayed as a barman in Wynyard, serving beers to simple people in a simple bar? What if I'd pursued my affair with Avril? All of these memories seemed so colourful and rich with possibilities, but for some reason they had seemed unsatisfying at the time. From where I was now slumped, with the nightmare that passed as my life, that fact seemed insane. It was hard to believe I had lived in that beautiful life and wandered away from it in search of this.

My memories were no longer any comfort at all. They were hideous for the loss they represented.

* * *

By now, Big Tiger had become comparatively slack when it came to the policing of drugs. More and more guards were taking advantage of the situation and the prisoners knew it. There was a healthy competition for the drug trade – guards were making money, prisoners were making money. It was madness to think that I was here because of heroin and I'd never seen so much of it in my life.

It seemed that nearly all foreigners were using heroin at this point. If they didn't, they were buying other drugs from either the guards or the hospital – Rohypnol, Valium and a variety of other tranquillisers. I was by now receiving money regularly from several different sources within my circle of family and friends. As dubious as it may sound, I was one of the lucky prisoners in that I could afford to keep myself away from the grinding pain of having to cope with the reality of Bang Kwang. I watched many less fortunate prisoners go mad from having to stay sober in this place. I remember one Portuguese prisoner who was fairly well adjusted for a time, but did not have the money to keep himself afloat. One night, out of the blue, he woke me to say that he had just been talking with his mother. For a moment I believed him, until I remembered where we were.

It turned out that, in desperation, the man had begged the doctors for some kind of pain killer. All they had been able to give him was some heavy anti-psychotic, the name of which I can't recall. I do remember that the generally accepted dose was 50 milligrams, and they had been giving him 200 milligrams. He had been straight for so long that this dosage had completely scrambled his mind. It was as if he'd had a lobotomy. He never came back.

* * *

Every once in a while, sensing that things were getting out of hand, the authorities in Bang Kwang would come down hard on the drug trade. A major crackdown would last for perhaps a couple of weeks, but the effect on the prisoners was devastating. The sound of hundreds of prisoners moaning in agony in the middle of the night is a sound that has to be heard to be believed.

It was after one of these periods that a guard approached me with the welcome news that he was carrying half a kilogram of pure heroin.

I purchased 350 grams from him, took it back to my cell and proceeded to divide it into small portions wrapped in 100 baht notes.

The next morning as we entered the yard, I was horrified to see that the guards were mounting a random search of the prisoners. I had all of these 100 baht packages of heroin stashed in my underpants. The guards and Blueboys were checking everything and there was no way for me to turn and retreat to my cell without arousing suspicion. I was surely done for.

Fortunately, the guard who had sold me the heroin in the first place was involved in the search. Upon seeing me approach, he stepped forward and declared to the others that he wished to search me personally. He roughly turned me around and began his search, then leaned forward and whispered in my ear that I must not say anything to arouse the suspicion of the other guards. He thrust his hand down the front of my pants and pretended to search around, eventually declaring to the others that he had found nothing of interest. I was then allowed to enter the yard.

I began to prepare my rig when a guard who had become suspicious stepped into the yard. He watched me closely for a few minutes as I sat like a wax dummy, pretending to be interested in the total nothingness of the yard.

As I looked around, I noticed a number of prisoners seemed to be interested in the same nothingness as I was. In a way, it was comical. The guard eventually wandered off and so began the most absurd flurry of activity in the yard, as every second prisoner produced his rig and began shooting up on the spot.

* * *

Life crept along. One day drifted into the next, lifeless and drugged. The only things that separated the days were occasional visits from missionaries and letters from home.

This long period of static was broken one morning when I was caught with heroin by one of the guards. The governor told me I was being sent to the *khun deo* – solitary confinement.

Since being in Bang Kwang, I had feared *khun deo* more than anything, but I still wasn't prepared for the shock. Cold and lonely and dark, it was more desolate than I had imagined. There seemed no space to even think, and yet there was not the basic comfort to sleep properly. I knew I would go mad in this hole.

I was also withdrawing from heroin.

It began slowly, with tremors and sweating and mild hallucinations. Then it worked its way into my brain. I began seeing things and was convinced I was being tormented by strange animals. The confinement of this tiny room closed in on me and I had no way of controlling my thoughts. My mind was consumed by a state of total outrage and panic. I simply could not last another minute. I had lost all will to survive or be happy again. I now just wanted my future and past to be finished and dead.

I unwrapped my sarong from my waist and twisted it into a thick rope, making a noose at one end. Looking up, I saw an exposed water pipe in the ceiling of the cell. I climbed onto the water trough and tied one end of the sarong to the pipe. Without giving myself time to think it through or change my mind, I placed my head in the noose and stepped free of the trough.

The noose tightened around my neck and I felt my throat stiffen. A sharp pain pulsed through my back and I knew I could not turn back now – I was going to die and I wanted that. I felt my bowels and my bladder give way and my head began to swim from lack of oxygen. It felt good to be letting go of everything.

Before I could lose consciousness, the sarong began to strain and rip under my weight. I reached up to stop it from tearing but it was too late and it ripped in half, dropping me to the floor on my knees. I immediately heaved the contents of my stomach onto the floor.

And there I stayed for the next few moments, on my knees in my own shit and vomit.

'No, no, no,' I murmured, wanting to cry but having no water for tears. I was too broken and pathetic to manage my own death. I couldn't die and I couldn't live. This was truly hell.

I picked myself up from the floor and began to clean myself with water from the trough. I didn't know what I was doing this for, as there was no reason to be clean.

'No, no, no,' I whispered, over and over for hours until my voice was completely gone.

* * *

I was to remain for one whole month in the *khun deo*, without so much as an aspirin. I had dysentery and what felt like pneumonia. I begged the guards for a doctor but they ignored me completely.

After a time, I learned that I could communicate with the other prisoners in solitary even though I couldn't see them. The actual cells were like dog kennels, separated by long walls that stretched out in front, making visual contact with other prisoners impossible. One night, however, when the guards had retired, I heard a fluttering noise outside my cell. When I looked, I saw that the prisoner in the cell next to me had thrown a length of string onto the floor, just within my reach. On the end of the string was a tennis ball. I heard the prisoner whisper to me, asking me to pass it on. I reached out and hauled in the ball, which I noticed had a small notch carved in it. Inside the ball was a letter for a prisoner in a cell down the end of the row. There was also a small pencil, for the prisoner's reply.

I reached out of my hatch and swung the ball to the next cell. This continued until the ball and its message had reached the cell it had been 'posted' to. Hours later, the ball bounced outside of my cell again, on its way back to the original sender.

This method was also used when prisoners were buying or selling drugs, which had been bought from corruptible guards.

Sometimes, the ball and string would bounce out of reach, and a prisoner would have to use a wet sarong to 'fish' for the string, until it was close enough to reach. This sometimes took hours and required excruciating patience. We had time.

I also learned how to boil my water in solitary. I got the recipe from the tennis ball.

There was a spoon that one of the prisoners had procured, into which he had drilled two holes. Somebody else had managed to get hold of some electrical wiring, from an old jug or something. By attaching one end of the wiring to the holes in the spoon, and the other end to the electrical fixtures in the light fitting that hung from the ceiling, it was possible to create a weak but effective element. The spoon could be placed in a jar or tin of water, which could be slowly brought to boil.

I remember thinking how strange it was that I had learned so many survival practices during my time in these prisons. This must have been what it was like for men at war. I remembered reading that during the Vietnam War, the Viet Cong would pounce on anything discarded by the American troops – a lighter here or an empty magazine cartridge there – and be able to turn the trash into something useful. This was the same sort of desperate living. A tennis ball, a piece of string, old electrical wires – Thailand's rubbish was keeping men alive in Bang Kwang.

* * *

Upon release from the *khun deo*, I became ill and was sent to the hospital. The doctor who examined me seemed to believe it was serious enough to have me transferred to Lard Yao for a time. This seemed odd to me, as I felt no worse than I had felt for a month. I had acclimatised to my own physical misery.

CHAPTER 11

LARD YAO

LARD YAO WAS MORE or less attached to Bang Kwang, but the feeling within the prison was entirely different. In some ways, it was worse.

Prisoners in Lard Yao were sick. I'm sure nearly every sickness in the world, both mental and physical, was represented within these walls. It was, in fact, a madhouse. The sound at night was like the soundtrack to a bad horror film. Sometimes, I was sure I could hear the sound of bodies dying, creaking as the life dragged itself out of them.

I was only meant to be here until I had fully or reasonably recovered, but an incident occurred very early on in my stay which would keep me in Lard Yao for the next nine months of my life.

One morning, they opened the cell of a German prisoner who had clearly lost his mind. He had been shouting and violently thrashing about in his cell. When the guards opened the door, the prisoner launched himself at them, throwing wild punches. The guards were totally surprised, and for a moment it looked as if the German was actually going to bash his way out of the prison. Within seconds, about 15 guards came dashing down the corridor and took to him with batons and canes. It didn't take them long to subdue him, and the German eventually collapsed under the force of the beating. But the guards didn't stop, continuing to thrash him as he lay prone on the ground. The other prisoners were standing around motionless, watching this display as if it were on television.

The guards continued to beat the prisoner until his bones were breaking and his skin began to burst. I just couldn't watch any more. I knew it was a stupid thing to do, but the ferocity of what I was watching just triggered a knee-jerk response. I simply could not stand here and watch this man be pulverised to death. I leaped in and started to pull the guards away from him, yelling at them to stop. I began shouting at the other prisoners to help me, but they just stood and watched.

My efforts were having no effect, with the guards simply pushing me away as they continued to pound the German into a bloody mass. I began to throw punches of my own. And that's when the guards turned.

One of the guards thumped me hard above the eye with his baton, sending me to the floor. I scrambled to my feet, not wanting to find myself in the same position as the German. Another strike to the head and I was down again. I raised my hands in terror and begged them to stop.

By now, with the German barely conscious, the guards' attention had shifted to me. I was petrified that I was about to undergo the same brutality I had just witnessed. But, right at that point, the building chief appeared. As I lay on the ground, the guards explained to him what had occurred, and the building chief ordered me to my feet. Seeing that I had felt such tremendous concern for the German prisoner, he said, I would now be responsible for his well-being. He then ordered that we both be put in punishment cells.

We were marched down to the end of the building. In fact, it was only me who was marched – the German was dragged by the feet. As they dragged him along the floor, they made sure that his head connected with any protruding object. They dragged him over an iron grill in the floor, his head shuddering over it as he went. They began laughing as they turned and dragged him over it two more times. The German was obviously unconscious – his bowels had relaxed and there was blood streaming from his ears – and there was no way that this punishment was of any use. It was simply to feed the spite of the guards.

When we reached the end of the building, they opened a cell and threw his body into it.

I was marched to the back of the building where chains were attached to my ankles. I was then taken to another cell not far away. I was horrified to see that the cell I was about to enter had no light in it at all, just a door and four walls. When I peered inside, I saw that there was a metal ring attached to the wall. The guards hustled me in and proceeded to attach one of the chains on my leg to this ring. They had only left me a few inches of slack and I pointed this out to them, stupidly thinking that they had made a mistake. The guards laughed and continued, leaving the cell when they had done. The door slammed shut and everything was black.

I couldn't move any more than a few inches, my leg married to the wall in this way. There was no bed in this room, just concrete floor. I tried to lie down but my leg was in the wrong position for me to do so. I could only sit against the wall in a half-squatting position. I could think of nothing but the shape of my body and the position I was in. I could see nothing. This was imprisonment at its most absolute.

* * *

The difficulty in telling this story – my whole story, in fact – is that there is no way for me to communicate duration of time to you. It may have taken a minute for you to have read of my position in this punishment cell, but I was in this position for a whole month. How do I convey that notion to you? There are no markers with which I can measure. The only way for you to come close to experiencing this is to read the previous paragraph over and over, every minute of every day, for a whole month. But nobody could do that without going mad with frustration.

* * *

Every morning, the guards opened the door, unchained me, and led me to the German prisoner's cell. The light hurt my eyes so much that I had to keep them practically closed the whole time. They gave me his rice and told me to take it in to him and put it on the floor, like food for a dog.

I couldn't see very well in the dark, but I could see well enough to know that they had virtually beaten this man to death. The way his face was misshapen indicated that they had broken his jaw in several places. His nose was twisted to one side and he was caked in his own dried blood. He just lay on the floor, making sounds that didn't seem natural.

I placed the rice near his mouth and urged him to eat, but that was ridiculous. He couldn't even lift his head from the floor. He tried to say something to me in English, but it made no sense. I realised he was going to die.

I remained in my cell with my leg chained to the ring on the wall. Eventually, they gave me a little more room on the chain, just enough movement to be able to reach the food that they'd push under the door once a day. One of the guards gave me a blanket, which provided some sort of protection from the hard concrete floor. The following day, I promised the guard a few packets of cigarettes if he could get me some more blankets. I rolled them together to make a bed, but the floor was still painfully hard. I had bruises on my hips and shoulders just from lying down. The toilet, the hole in the ground, festered under my nose. I tried to ration the water in the bucket, but I had to use most of it to wash after using the toilet. Once, I ran out of water too early and, weak with thirst, begged the guard for more. He told me that was just tough.

In darkness such as this, you develop night eyes, and objects become mere shapes that are defined only by the varying shades of black. Sometimes, it seemed I could see phantom shapes. I could make out the bowl that held my food, even when it was not there, simply by looking at the area in which it was usually placed.

One night, I opened my eyes and could see a new shape in the cell. It was large and moving, like a black cloud. As my eyes widened, I realised that it was another person. This cell was scarcely big enough for one, but they had placed another prisoner in here with me overnight. He, too, was chained to the wall, but we still found it difficult to avoid each other.

* * *

Upon release from Lard Yao, I returned to Bang Kwang and was allowed to remove the chains that had been on my ankles for nine months. There had been a significant change in Bang Kwang during my absence. Prisoners were now allowed to attend 'contact visits'. These were visits from regular people – strangers, really – who simply wanted to make contact with prisoners in Big Tiger. They would see a list of names, with the nationality of the prisoner next to the name, and choose who they wanted to see. These visits were conducted on a stretch of lawn off to the right of the doorway to the punishment cells. The guards sometimes used this small field as an oval on which they would play soccer while the prisoners looked on. It was during one of these visits that I met Mr and Mrs Charles Holmes, English Baptist missionaries who spent a large part of their lives visiting prisoners and trying to help them spiritually. I don't know if I've met such selfless people either before or since. They would bring me food from the outside and do their best to organise anything else I might require. They began to visit regularly. The only thing they asked in return is that I try to familiarise myself with the Bible, a copy of which they gave to me. They suggested that a fine place to start would be the Book of Daniel, where the central figure is a man who is left overnight in a den of lions, but survives through his faith in God.

Reading the Bible, I found it to be a book of untold violence and torture, where the victims are usually those who transgressed God's law. It was only when they repented that the love of God was exposed to them in all its might.

One chapter which particularly intrigued me was the Book of Job. In it, God forces Job, his faithful servant, to endure unspeakable hardship and loss. The reason God did this was because Satan made him a wager that Job could be made to turn against God.

Of course, I saw that Job and I had a lot in common. So too did I have much in common with God and Satan.

We were all punters.

CHAPTER 12

MUTINY

IT HAPPENED ON Sunday, 5 August 1985.

On this day, I was involved in a contact visit with a girl called Simone. She was from the northern beaches in Sydney, was on a working holiday in Thailand and had simply wanted to meet an Australian prisoner. She was only 19 and I had been visited a few times by her. After so long without female contact, it was easy to get attached to a person like Simone. On this day, I was so enthralled by her company that it took me a while before I realised what was happening.

There was a panic rippling through the guards. They seemed to be moving about quickly and whispering orders to each other. I looked up at the tower that stood on the outer wall and was alarmed to see that guns – M16s – were being thrown to the guards below.

Suddenly, guards were everywhere on the grass oval, hustling visitors out to the caged area beyond the yard. A guard picked Simone up off the grass and whisked her away before we could say goodbye. Something big was happening and nobody seemed to know what it was.

Guards began rushing into the yard and shouting at us, telling us to return to our cells. I found Paul and he was as bewildered as I.

When we entered our cell, the guards locked it behind us. They did the same with every cell in the building.

Word eventually filtered through. Someone in Building Six had taken a guard from behind and held him hostage with a knife. It was said that several other prisoners had taken his gun and were threatening other guards.

At first, the whole affair was tremendously exciting. The guards in Big Tiger had never dealt with a situation like this and we were all curious to see how it would turn out. But an hour passed without news. The silence was deafening.

After a time, we realised that we hadn't seen or heard from a guard in hours. There was the sound of a commotion in the distance, but it didn't sound like a battle of any sort – more like a flurry of excitement, as one might hear in a children's playground.

Just then, there was a tremendous crashing sound further down the hall of the building, like somebody trying to bash their way through a door. Then the sound doubled. Then tripled.

A figure appeared at the gate of our cell. It was not a guard, but a prisoner. He began to smash the lock on our cell with a piece of pipe. This was happening everywhere, he said. There was a riot. The guards were all gone. Big Tiger was under siege from the inside.

Every door in Building Five had been smashed. There were prisoners running everywhere, wrecking everything they could see. It was absolute mayhem.

Paul and I didn't know what to do. It was impossible not to get swept up in the excitement of it all, but we knew there was no way that this could end in the prisoners' favour. We would all surely be executed.

Prisoners had broken into the guards' quarters and even the governor's office. They had taken down pictures of the king and were storming around, holding the king above their heads, chanting and screaming as if they were out of their minds. One prisoner told me that it was all because of the news that the Thai government had announced that they were going to put a stop to the King's Pardon, the process by which a prisoner could be released much earlier than his sentence decreed.

Suddenly, a voice boomed over the public address system. The voice told us to stop the riot and return to our cells or we would be punished. The prisoners either shouted abuse back at the voice or ignored it completely. For the first time since this ordeal started, I was frightened. I had once been told of a riot that had occurred in Bang Kwang some ten years earlier. Everyone was shot. I truly believed that the current authorities of Bang Kwang would not hesitate to execute the lot of us.

That night, the prisoners of Big Tiger raged. It was manic. Somebody had stolen one of the guards' tape-recorders and music was booming through the prison. Sometime during the evening, the prison went wild to the sound of 'All Along The Watchtower', by Jimi Hendrix.

The whole scene was surreal and terrifying at the same time. Paul and I just wandered around the prison. Nobody slept that night.

In one room in Building Five, we came across a small cell where five Thais sat in a circle. They had candles burning and appeared to be praying. The scene was a little oasis of serenity in all of this madness, and so Paul and I moved in to join them.

I asked one of the Thais what he was praying for, and he replied that they were asking for their souls to be blessed.

'For tomorrow,' he said, 'we will all die.'

Dawn of the next morning saw a chilling quiet fall over Big Tiger. There could be no doubt that the authorities would put a stop to the riot today, but there was no sign of any guards, police or officials. There was just silence, occasionally broken by another shout of elation from somewhere in the prison. Most of the foreigners were hiding in the red rooms. I stayed with Paul and two Americans towards the back of the building. We just lay there in silence, keeping an eye on the prison walls and the front gate for signs of action.

It was mid-morning when the storm finally broke. It all happened at once. The doors of the prison burst open and soldiers charged in. They were troops from the army Special Forces and they were firing blindly. Helicopters seemed to rise out of the earth beyond the walls of the prison. Commandos were coming over the walls and positioning themselves, as if waiting for the order to attack. There was lots of firing and it was deafening. My heart was pounding.

I saw one prisoner run towards the wall and his body was cut to pieces by gunfire. Soldiers were shooting down on the yard from the stepways along the walls of the prison.

Edward, one of the Americans, claimed the soldiers were shooting blanks, as to fire real bullets in this difficult strategic position would be to risk firing upon themselves. Just as these words left his lips, a Thai prisoner a few metres away had his chest blown apart.

Across the yard, I could see a prisoner scaling the wall. He was halfway up when his body went limp and he fell to the ground.

Edward began to panic. He took off his shirt and stood waving it above his head. He then began walking towards the wall, shouting that he wanted to talk to the officials. The soldiers levelled their rifles at him and for a split second I winced as I was sure he was about to be cut down. They shouted at him to go back and lie down.

Just then, a soldier appeared behind us. He jammed the muzzle of his M16 into the back of my head and screamed at me not to move. I lay there trembling as the gun remained at my head. A guard who knew us appeared and told the soldier that we were harmless. The soldier removed the gun from my head, but told me to take my shirt off, lie face down on the ground with my hands behind my head and not move until I was told to do otherwise.

After about an hour, the firing had ceased. Prisoners were being rounded up and herded around the prison by shouting soldiers. The terror among us was intense. Every prisoner had his hands tied behind his back with twine. I noticed that some of the twine was red and some was white and I wondered about the meaning of this.

Suddenly, a group of about five prisoners were brought forward and made to kneel on the ground. Before I had time to wonder about what was happening, the soldiers raised their rifles to the backs of the prisoners' heads and shot them dead. Then more prisoners were brought forward. I noticed that they all had their hands tied with red twine.

It was all happening so quickly. As more shots rang out and more bodies fell, terrified prisoners began turning to others and asking to be told what colour string their hands were tied with.

Paul and I and several other foreigners were led into the lower reaches of Building Five. The sewer had exploded and there was a massive pool of sewage inches thick on the floor.

A soldier then commanded that we get down on our bellies and crawl through it, as punishment for being a part of the Bang Kwang riot.

An Australian called Bruce refused. He turned to the soldier and said that he had nothing to do with the riot and would not be punished for it. He had been a good prisoner and had remained in his cell the entire time the riot was taking place.

The soldier glared at Bruce, and for a moment I thought he'd made a fatal mistake. But, to my surprise, the soldier told him to step aside and ordered the rest of us to get down and crawl through the shit.

A Thai prisoner, no doubt spurred on by Bruce's show of defiance, declared that he too was going to refuse. Without hesitation, the soldier brought the butt of his M16 crashing against the side of the Thai's head. The force of the blow was astonishing. Making a rude blurting sound, the Thai's head just split apart, like a watermelon that had been dropped from a height. He fell into the pool, his blood and brains spilling into the shit.

The soldier shouted at us to get down and crawl, and we did.

* * *

Paul was badly beaten during the riot. He could barely walk, his right leg buckled and broken from the shin down. We had been locked in our cell – all 36 of us – for three days with no food and no medical attention at all. Paul was in agony.

On the third day after the riot was put down, they finally opened the door of our cell and ordered us to come out and wash. Myself and one of the Americans had our arms around Paul, helping him along as he found walking impossible. Tempers were incredibly strained, and one of the guards began barking at us to move faster. We explained that Paul had damaged his leg, that the nerves had been destroyed and he could move no faster. The guard brought his cane stinging down onto our backs and told us to move faster.

From now on, Bang Kwang was going to be more uncompromising than ever before.

CHAPTER 13

LIFE

LOOKING BACK ON IT NOW, I realise that much of life in Bang Kwang was spent creating a world as similar to the one we knew on the outside as possible. We had forgotten what it was like to live in the real world, to the point where we would refer to events in outside society as if it were another state of the universe. We referred to things that occurred 'outside in the world'. We were not in the world at all. But, somewhere deep down, we longed for the heartbreakingly commonplace, the way of life in a regular community. And, as best we could, we transformed the happenings in Big Tiger into a pathetic model of our former lives.

We did business and kept accounts. We kept track of each others' social-and financial standing. Mr and Mrs Holmes had given me a diary, in which I kept daily records of the commerce of Big Tiger.

'Must give Paul 1,500 baht today . . . David owes me 500 baht . . . Three Star gave me one pill, owes me another two . . . Ronald and I will go back to our old way of keeping accounts today . . .'

As in any community, alliances were made and displayed. During my last years in Bang Kwang, I formed a network of close friends and we tried to stick together.

One of them was a man called Gary Genovese, an Italian–American whose uncle was the Don of the Genovese crime family in New York. Gary told me that either he or his brother were next in line for the top job. It was strange to think of how such a powerful crime family could not bring pressure on the more than corruptible Thai authorities. But Gary believed his time in Bang Kwang would simply prove his mettle to those in New York. His brother, Bob, was also in a prison in the United States.

One day, Gary showed me a photo his brother had sent him. It featured Bob standing with his arm around a reasonably attractive girl. Apparently, he had met her in the prison, which was low-security and in which the prisoners were occasionally allowed to mix with the inmates of the nearby women's prison.

The inscription on the back of the photo read:

'Dear brother Gary,
This girl and I are soon going to be married. And guess what? She's a murderer!'

* * *

Diary 6 June 1986

Was sent to *khun deo* this day. They busted Gary Genovese with a needle. We eat together so we both got sent to solitary confinement. Do not like solitary – very hard time.

* * *

There was an Italian boy in Bang Kwang called Marcello. Not many people liked him – he used to get high and dance around like a ballerina in his underwear. This prison had clearly turned him into something else.

While spending time in solitary, Marcello developed pneumonia. After he was released from the *khun deo*, he staggered over one morning to see the doctor. He was obviously delirious and the doctor knew he was very ill, but all he could do was lay him on a bed, which was nothing more than a few boards and a blanket.

I can't remember why I was in the hospital, but I was situated on a bed not far from Marcello's. A few days later I received a visit from the embassy and with them was an Australian doctor. I asked the doctor if he could step outside the boundaries of procedure for a moment and take a look at Marcello. The doctor said he would.

He came back 20 minutes later with an ashen look on his face and asked to see the head prison doctor. Marcello, he said, would surely die if he did not receive proper medical attention within 24 hours.

The following evening, Marcello began hallucinating. He'd lost control of his bowels and he was lying in a sea of shit. He saw me watching him, lifted his hand to wave and there was excrement dripping from his fingers.

In the morning, I asked a Thai to help me push Marcello's bed over to the water trough so we could wash him. I tipped water all over his body and did my best to get him as clean as I could. He managed to peep through his delirium to utter the words, 'Thank you'.

I remember Paul being somewhat surprised that I'd done this, as Marcello was considered such a bastard by all foreigners in the prison. But, to me, it was important not to become like the guards – desensitised and without compassion. After everything I'd seen, I still couldn't bring myself to be a robot.

As it turned out, the Australian doctor who had seen Marcello had contacted the Italian embassy and informed them of his condition. The Italian embassy sent a doctor with a parcel of drugs and medicines, but it arrived too late. The previous evening Marcello had passed away during the night, drowning in his own phlegm.

Later in the day, during visiting, I saw a representative from the Italian embassy and approached him. I asked if he had heard about Marcello, and he replied that he had and was on his way to see him in a moment.

Right then, the truck containing Marcello's body began to pull out of the prison.

'See that truck?' I pointed. 'I'm afraid Marcello's in there.'

The Italian looked for a moment before realising what I had said. Then he did the strangest thing. Exclaiming loudly, he jumped from his chair and ran after the truck, chasing it as it lumbered towards the gate. He was still running when the truck pulled out and the gates slammed closed behind it. He stopped, turned around and walked back towards us, as distraught as a father who'd just seen his dead son taken away.

Marcello did not have a family and so was buried in unholy ground, in some place outside the cemetery.

I'm so glad we washed him.

* * *

Diary 27 April 1986

Steve came back today, but maybe cannot come to see me until 7 May. Says he will be here before the 7th – I'm sure he'll be here on the 6th with the Holmeses. At least, I hope so. I should have spoken more today. Next time I'll make up for it.

* * *

Diary 6 May 1986

Mr and Mrs Charles Holmes and Steve will be back on this day. I'm looking forward to Steve coming to see me again.

Must think of some more things to talk about – keep his interest in me. Also I must complete all Bible study forms and give them to Charles. Must also complete food list.

* * *

Diary 7 May 1986
This date could be wrong. Said they'd be back to visit on 6/5/86, but this must be wrong. They might come any day this week, even today.

* * *

Diary 9 May 1986
Maybe the Holmeses and Steve will be here today, Friday. Anyway, as long as they come this week, everything will be okay.

* * *

One day I was lining up to see a doctor when a French prisoner came dashing into the office. He was hysterical, going through withdrawal from heroin. He cried to the doctor, begging him for something to ease the pain. The doctor said that he could do nothing for him. The Frenchman then replied that if he did not get something now, he would commit suicide.

Upon hearing this, the doctor opened his top drawer and removed a knife. He then held it towards the Frenchman, handle first, and told him to please commit suicide out in the corridor, as he did not want a mess in his office.

At this point in time, such events struck me as humorous. After a while, you start to see humour in the darkness. You laugh at the blackest things. It's the only way to get by.

I returned to my cell to tell Paul about what I had just seen, but found him not to be there. I asked another prisoner where he was and he said that he had been taken away by the guards. Later, I was to discover that Paul had been transferred to Lard Yao permanently. Due to the overcrowding of Bang Kwang, all foreign prisoners serving 30 years or less were to be transferred to Lard Yao.

I was heartbroken to hear this. Since climbing on to the plane at Sydney airport all those years ago, Paul and I had been together. For me, he had become a brother. We'd seen each other through more than most people go through in their lives.

I was not to realise that I would never see Paul again in Thailand. And I would never again see the Paul that I knew. Ever.

* * *

Diary 20 December 1986
I miss Paul so very much. I hope he is okay. Paul Hayward is my case partner, but more than this he is my best friend. I love and miss him so terribly much. I wish he was still in here with me. It's a real pain in the heart. We've been in this prison together for eight years and we've been through everything, things other people have not endured. Now, we've been separated – he's been moved to Klong Prem Central Prison. I think our friendship is the best. We know what we've both been through – hell, many times over. Our friendship is built on strength of character. We know each other's heart and mind.

* * *

There was a pig farm in Bang Kwang. The pigs were bigger than the prisoners. They ate the same as we did, but appeared to be getting second helpings.

Thai prisoners worked on the pig farm for a pitiful wage, but they had learned of a way to supplement their income . . .

Many people have asked me about sex in Bang Kwang, and whether sex and rape were regular occurrences among the prisoners, as it is within many Western prisons. I have to say that it isn't the case. Thais frown heavily on rape, and are not tolerant of homosexuality. There were prisoners who were known to be homosexual, and the authorities were wise enough to put them together in their own little clusters in Big Tiger. In a prison as crowded as this, romantic interludes were neither possible, welcome or wise.

And so, the pig farm became something of a brothel. For a few packets of cigarettes, a Bang Kwang pig would 'love you long time'. Many Thais partook of this service, but the foreigners found it naturally repulsive.

The amusing thing was that, to the Thais, the fact that you were having sex with a pig did not mean that you had to abandon your strict heterosexual tendencies. Sex with a male pig would cost two packets of cigarettes, whereas the price for sex with a female pig rose sharply to five packets. Presumably, a few more packets and you could pick and choose between a wider variety of female pigs.

After all, you wouldn't want to get an ugly one.

* * *

Diary 20 February 1988
Today is a holiday – Makha Bucha Day, whatever that is. I only know that everything is closed. No hospital, no visits, no fucking nothing. Everything just stops. This country has so many fucking public holidays it's not funny. They have a holiday for just about anything. Crazy. But, to me in here, it's just another normal day. Another wasted day in my life.

* * *

Sometimes, the embassy would send us magazines. Most of the time they were *Women's Weekly*, or something like that. It was exciting to see something from the outside world, but generally made for unsatisfying reading. They were usually about one year old, and the guards had gone through and removed any pictures they thought might give us ideas: a gun, a helicopter, a story about somebody beating the odds. Sometimes they simply removed photos that they knew would give us too much joy. The women's fashion section was full of holes. We'd read stories about how some beautiful young starlet was making it in the big time, but the photo would be cut from the page.

One time, a girl who was visiting me produced a pornographic magazine – *Playboy* or *Penthouse* – and said she'd like to give it to me. We had a good guard that day and I asked him if he could help us. I paid him a few packets of cigarettes to smuggle the magazine in for us, which he did.

I'd seen magazines like this before, but that was many years before and the morality of the times had clearly changed while I had been incarcerated. The women in this magazine were astonishingly beautiful. The poses they struck were unbelievable.

The next few days saw the magazine moving through our section of the prison like a best seller. Prisoners were paying top dollar to see it. It became such an issue that eventually some of the guards began asking if they could borrow 'The Book'. The Thais couldn't believe that such beautiful Western women could behave like they did in this magazine, for all to see. Some of them had never seen a woman naked in their lives.

Sadly, the guards destroyed The Book. This time, however, their destruction was not intentional – it was a sad day for them too when The Book died. It was simply a case of over-use.

One afternoon, a girl came to visit me and, in the middle of our conversation, asked me when I had last had sex. I told her it was many years ago. She said she wished she could get me out. It was so long since anyone had said anything like that to me that I actually spent a long time wondering what she meant.

Later in the conversation, she told me that she had a tattoo and asked if I would like to see it. With that, she pulled up her dress and revealed a small tattoo on her backside. I nodded my approval and she sat down to continue our conversation, unaware of the fact that I was on fire from what I had just seen. Some minutes later, unable to get her backside out of my mind, I asked her if I could inspect that tattoo again, mumbling something about my interest in the artwork. She stood and raised her dress again and I sat stupefied, feigning interest in the detail of the tattoo. She finally realised what was happening when she looked around to see a cluster of guards standing around behind me. To this day, I don't know what the tattoo depicted.

I think a lot of women get some sort of perverse thrill from the idea of men in prison. I remember one girl who offered to sell a prisoner her panties for 500 baht. He was more than happy to part with the money, and convinced a guard to collect them for him. News spread quickly in the visiting yard and within minutes this girl was sitting there talking to about 20 prisoners with monstrous erections.

The guards disposed of the panties, however. While they enjoyed The Book, they couldn't understand how anybody could get any joy out of another person's underpants.

* * *

Certain prisoners with a good rating were allowed extraordinary privileges. One man, an Australian called John, was allowed to build a house in the common section. He built it out of scrap and pieces of wood which he purchased from the Thais. It was quite a masterpiece.

Bruce, the Australian who refused to crawl through the sewer after the riot, was well known to be fond of the cats that populated Big Tiger. He fed them and looked after them and they swarmed around him as he moved through the prison. He was like the Birdman of Alcatraz, only with cats.

One day, one of the cats had kittens and the authorities allowed Bruce to keep them in his cell and tend to them. He had a wooden box in the corner of the cell, which served as a nest.

Naturally, the kittens had little chance of survival in a place like Big Tiger, and eventually only one kitten remained.

Determined to keep this kitten alive, Bruce watched over it day and night. For weeks he could be seen cradling the kitten in his hands, eating with it at meal times, playing with it in the yard. He bathed it and fed it with his own food. It was an unusual sight – this tough man doting over a tiny kitten as if it were his child, and all framed by the squalor of Bang Kwang. But everybody understood his attachment to the kitten. In this place, anything that provided you with joy became the critical focus of your life. To have a small, living creature dependent on you, and returning your care with affection, was nothing short of a dream. We were deeply envious of Bruce.

After a time, the kitten began to grow. Bruce organised for people on the outside to send him provisions which the kitten required. One day, he received a parcel containing tins of proper cat food. Some of the other prisoners were upset by this, and spoke of how Bruce's kitten was eating better than they were. But Bruce warned that the tins of food were strictly for the kitten and anyone who stole them would have to deal with him personally.

One day, Bruce left the kitten sleeping in the wooden box in the corner of the cell as he went to visit the hospital, in which animals were not allowed. When he returned, he found several Thais sitting in his cell, smiling. He looked at the wooden box and saw that the kitten was gone. Then he saw it. The kitten was suspended from a piece of string tied to a bolt in the wall. The string had been pulled so tight around the kitten's neck that its tongue protruded. Its eyes were squeezed shut, as if in pain. Bruce was so devastated he collapsed on the floor of the cell and sobbed. The Thais then cut the kitten down, skinned it and ate it until all that was left was bone.

* * *

Bruce never got over this incident, withdrawing completely from other prisoners. Eventually, he was released and returned to his home in Melbourne. I wrote to him several times but got no reply. I did, however, receive a letter from Bruce's mother. It was not good news.

Upon Bruce's return, she said, he had appeared to adjust well for a time, and seemed to be getting used to life as it had been before. He spoke very little of his experiences in Bang Kwang, and she had understood this as nothing more than a desire to forget the past.

One day, Bruce returned from a trip to the corner store looking pale and bothered. His mother asked him what was wrong but he didn't answer. He simply ambled into his bedroom, locked the door and refused to come out for weeks.

Bruce's mother was writing this letter nearly six months after the incident, and she was sorry to report that, since that day, Bruce was yet to utter a word.

* * *

Diary 4 April 1988
Solitary confinement. My body is in solitary but my mind and soul are free. They will never be able to incarcerate my mind and will. In October, I will have served ten years. A decade. How little people know or care.

I'm so very, very hungry, but I've been hungry for ten years. I dream of food. Oh, God, I dream of eating decent food again. Five days now with no food. I'm living on water. River water, I think, from the brown, muddy mass of a river outside the prison.

How much there is for me to tell. I pray that God will continue to bless and watch over me, as I must tell of my experiences. For now, only God knows how much I've suffered. To think that in this day and age, man, with all his technology, allows places like this, where the clock of progress has stopped. I must survive and get free, so I can tell the world exactly what's happening. And by God's grace I will. For through God I have been blessed. It is His will, all that I've lived through. It must have a far greater meaning. Soon, the world will know. Praise God that I can still love.

The bugs are driving me crazy.

* * *

One morning, a guard opened the door of my cell and told me to collect my things, for I was being released in an hour. I couldn't believe it. I became giddy and weak with excitement at the thought of this nightmare being finally over.

I rolled up my bed and sat, thinking of what I would be doing in a few days' time. I became so caught up in these thoughts that I didn't even notice that more than an hour had passed since being told of my release. Another hour passed. I sat and waited.

Eventually, the guard reappeared. He had a wicked smile on his face and at first I thought it may have been the usual goodbye smile that this particular guard dished out. I had never liked him during my time in Bang Kwang. Today, however, he was my favourite guard, and I was prepared to let him get away with anything. It only took me a few moments to realise what was happening: it was a trick. The guard had simply wanted to destroy my day by giving me false deliverance. I was not being released today, or any other day in the foreseeable future.

I entered the yard and sat, watching the others who, like me, had nothing to keep them alive but fear of dying.

* * *

Diary 15 June 1988
Today the embassy came to the hospital with Dr Brody, who gave

me a good physical examination. He said I was holding my own –
the glands in my neck haven't got any worse. Apart from that, he
said I'm quite healthy, under the circumstances.

* * *

For years, madness was all around me. You might see a man on the
street who is a lunatic and you'd think that was something of a
novelty. Big Tiger had such people as its population. They were my
neighbours, the people I interacted with.

One day, a German prisoner jumped up and declared, with no
invitation or provocation whatsoever, that Hitler was a genius, that
the final solution was a good idea and that it was a tremendous
shame Germany did not win the Second World War. The Thais
simply watched in bewilderment – there aren't too many Jewish
Thais and I doubt they even knew who Hitler was. Frustrated by the
lack of response, the German began shouting that we'd all know
what he was talking about when the Fourth Reich came along. Then
he began to march around the prison, goose-stepping like a Nazi
Gestapo officer.

An Australian prisoner had finally seen and heard enough.

'Hey, Adolf!' he shouted.

The sound of that name threw the German into a state of intense
excitement. He began saluting and shouting 'Sieg Heil!' The
Australian marched up to him and struck him so hard that his nose
ripped apart, half of it flapping from the side of his face as he
dropped to the floor.

One night, I found a young Swiss prisoner sobbing in the cell. I
went over to speak to him and he told me he wanted to die, that he
couldn't stand another day in this place. When I asked how long he
had to serve in Bang Kwang, he replied that he was to be released in
six months. I told him that he was crazy, that he need only hold on
for a short time. I had another 20 years.

Much later in the evening, I awoke to find that he had overdosed. I tried to wake him, but realised he was close to death. I called for the guards and asked them to please take him to the hospital. They entered the cell and removed him, but simply laid him outside the cell and left him. I just stood and watched him die.

One morning, a guard came to tell me that I was moving to another section of the prison – Building 7/1. It was for foreign prisoners who had infectious diseases. Apparently, tests had shown that I had developed hepatitis.

I would remain in Building 7/1 for the duration of my life in Bang Kwang.

* * *

Diary 22 March 1989
American Embassy came today with good news for David. David should be going home by the middle of next month, back to New York. I will miss him very much. We'll keep in contact. I hope that one day we will meet outside.

* * *

One night I dreamed of voices. They were chattering away to each other in a strange, high-pitched tone. They became so loud that I eventually awoke. But the voices were still chattering.

When I opened my eyes I saw something that made me feel mad.

Above me were three small creatures that I find impossible to describe. They were ugly and evil and glaring down at me in the dark. Their mouths were moving, but they were not synchronised with the voices I could hear. I couldn't make out everything being said, but I did hear the word 'ready'.

I closed my eyes, hoping that I would wake and find that the visions and the voices were gone. But when I opened my eyes, the creatures had come closer. They were descending upon me. I closed my eyes again and when I opened them the creatures were gone and it was quiet.

I knew now that I was going insane.

Just then, a Thai prisoner touched me on the shoulder. He had been praying in the corner of the cell, he said, when he had raised his head and looked in my direction. He said he had seen three tiny figures of Buddha floating in the air above me. He said they were here to protect me and not to be afraid of them. He went back to his corner and continued with his prayers.

I didn't sleep for the rest of the night. I just lay there trying to fathom the idea that the world was insane and not me.

* * *

Diary 7 April 1989
Paul is supposed to be released today. I wonder how he feels, going home after 11 years of prison. He should never have done so much time – it's so unfair. I should have done the time for both of us, as I've done more wrong than Paul. This was Paul's first scam. He should've done a maximum of two years, not this long. I hope he copes all right.

* * *

Paul was hustled out of Lard Yao prison at two o'clock in the morning. I was overwhelmed with happiness for him, but I was also worried about what he would find when he returned home. Sometime before, we had been visited by a journalist from a Sydney newspaper who was doing a story on Paul. The journalist was sympathetic towards Paul, but in no way defensive of Paul's actions. The story was simply the tale of a man who had everything and destroyed it by making one unforgivable yet tragic mistake.

After the story appeared, the newspaper was flooded with

letters, many of them sympathetic. But I heard that a good half of them were damning, chastising the newspaper for wasting space on a criminal, incriminating Paul as a wicked role-model for their children to have to hear about and basically declaring their belief that he should have been hanged.

Paul would have to face this when he returned to Australia, and I didn't know how he'd cope. Had we been released together, it might have been all right. As a team, we might have had the strength to combat the attackers, just as we had in these prisons. Alone, neither of us was as strong.

* * *

I remember the last time I had any fun at all in Big Tiger.

A group of us had banded together to pool resources in order to make some wine. Somebody had worked out how to brew it by using pineapple. Another prisoner had procured a tin garbage can and some plastic. A few of the guards had been bribed to turn a blind eye as the can sat in the corner of the room with the fermenting liquid inside.

Then one day it was announced that some high-ranking Thai authorities were coming to inspect the prison. The governor approached us and warned us to behave during the visit. We represented him, he said, and if we were polite to the authorities he would reward us.

Before the inspection, we disguised the can as best we could, covering it with sarongs so that it looked like nothing more than a piece of furniture.

When the authorities came, we stood in the door of our open cell like schoolboys on parade. The governor approached with the authorities, who were resplendent in their immaculate military uniforms. We were introduced as 'the best foreigners in the building'.

Apparently impressed with the cleanliness of our cell, the most official of the authorities entered and began looking around. The governor followed right behind him, obviously nervous about what he might find.

Suddenly, as if by an act of God, there came a strange burbling noise from the can in the corner. Then, to the combined horror of all, it exploded, spattering the governor and the immaculately attired authorities in a shower of sticky yellow sludge.

Not even the dour Thai authorities could resist laughing at the complete absurdity of God's timing. This was the last thing I saw that made me smile in Bang Kwang.

What followed was a condensed trail of sadness so blunt and repetitive that I have almost cast the feelings from my mind.

* * *

By the middle of 1989 I had begun to feel almost comfortable in the rotten world of Big Tiger. No doubt I'd just acclimatised to the madness, but I think it mostly had to do with the friendships I had made. For the first time since I had arrived in Bangkok, I felt as if I could survive it.

The forces that had governed my life for the last ten years must have sensed this feeling of mine from somewhere in the universe, and they began to act.

Leo Odems was a big black American who had become friends with Ronald, David, Gary and myself. He was so full of life it was impossible not to be swept up in it. Even the guards liked him. When he was in the *khun deo*, the guards looking in on him would tell him to smile, as they couldn't see him in the dark. The guards never failed to laugh as Leo's widest grin shone out at them from the blackness of the cell.

Leo and I became very close. I knew he was due to leave the prison before me, and he gave me his address in New York. He told me never to lose it, for when I got out of Big Tiger, we would meet in America and make up for the life we had wasted in prison.

Imagining what it would be like to be in America with Leo, I found myself almost glad that I had come to Bang Kwang. I wouldn't have crossed his path otherwise.

One night, Leo overdosed on heroin. We slapped him around, woke him and got him to the doctor in what appeared to be enough time for his life to be saved. But, having been brought back to consciousness, Leo began to haemorrhage.

He lay crying in my arms, begging me not to let him die.

And then he died.

Diary 5 May 1989
Embassy told me today that I am top priority for a King's Pardon . . . David and I share a room only big enough for one person. It's just David and myself now. When he goes, I'll be truly alone.

* * *

Diary 8 May 1989
David did go home today at 4 p.m.

* * *

Diary 13 May 1989
There are only three of us in this section now – myself, Ronald Burnett and Christian Gippett. David went home on Monday. The three of us are eating together – before, we ate alone. The feeling is good between us.

* * *

I got to know Ronald Burnett, an American who had fought in Vietnam. While he and members of his platoon were crouched in a bunker, a mortar shell had burst, killing all but Ron. He was critically injured and was sent to Japan to recover in hospital. For months he languished in bed, doped senseless on morphine, not knowing quite where he was. Eventually he was released and sent back to America. By then, of course, he had become addicted to morphine. For a time he tried to kick the addiction, but it proved too strong. Unable to obtain morphine easily, Ron turned to a more available alternative: heroin.

His addiction to heroin had brought him to Thailand in search of a cheaper supply. He was arrested with a large quantity of the drug and that is how he came to be in Bang Kwang.

We became very close, then he was released.

* * *

Diary 13 September 1989
Today is my birthday. I will be 36 years old. I came to prison when I was 25. Far too long. I've wasted my youth in a hell hole.

* * *

I'd known Christian vaguely while we were in the main body of the prison, but I got to know him well when we were the last of the foreigners in our section.

He was French and had been in jails all over the world, always for drugs. He was heavily addicted to heroin.

The French embassy were good to their people in Bang Kwang. Christian enjoyed a constant supply of medicines and good food, which he was always happy to share with me.

One day, the embassy gave him 100 tablets of Rohypnol, Christian's preferred legal drug. He was particularly generous in sharing them with me, for he had another delivery arriving on this day.

Christian had organised with a Thai to have an ounce of smack brought into the prison, in bags concealed in the intestines of a pig. A delivery for Christian of animal entrails would not have aroused suspicion among the guards, for he was constantly being sent parcels of exotic food.

That afternoon, the parcel arrived. But when Christian retreated to his cell to remove the heroin, he found that the bags had burst and the heroin had mixed with the blood and juices of the pig's insides.

When I saw him that evening, he was desperately disappointed. He needed heroin badly. I suggested that he take some Rohypnol and go to sleep. In the morning, we'd think of something.

Before returning to his cell, he left a large quantity of Rohypnol on my bed for me. Looking back, it was too large a quantity. Without the heroin, Christian would have needed every one of those tablets over the next few weeks.

The following morning, the guards shook me awake and told me that there was something wrong with Christian. I ran to his cell and saw him lying there, a needle poking out of his arm. Beside him was the bag of pig's entrails. Christian had been injecting the juice from intestines, hoping to get a hit from the heroin that had dissolved inside.

I raised his upper body from the floor and began shaking him, begging him not to die. Blood spilled from his ear as if it had been bottled. His body was cold and stiff.

I couldn't let go of Christian. I kept telling him he wasn't dead.

I looked up to the ceiling and asked God how much more of this shit he wanted me to see.

'How much more, God?' I cried out. One of the guards started to sob.

* * *

Diary 21 September 1989
Christian's body found this morning when they opened the door.

Brain haemorrhage. Had to break his bones to get him out of the room . . . Oh, please, let this year be my year. I don't think I can do much more of this. It's really starting to wear me down.

* * *

When Christian died, I stopped taking heroin. I was so utterly destroyed emotionally that I scarcely felt the withdrawals. I was too engrossed in the misery that the real world had delivered me. My King's Pardon now looked unlikely and I could barely listen to the embassy officials when they referred to it. If my King's Pardon were to be refused, I would have to wait another four years to apply again. I was beginning to consider the very real possibility that I would die in this prison, and that thought caused my mood to fluctuate wildly between a state of unbearable panic and total ambivalence. There was no middle ground between these two states of mind.

Everyone who had touched my life in a positive way was gone. My brother, my father, Leo, Christian. My mother and Paul and Ronald and David and Gary Genovese – all of them were so far out of reach they may as well have ceased to exist for me.

I was unbelievably close to death. I was actually dead already. A piece of meat who just happened to be able to think.

* * *

Diary 25 December 1989
Today is Christmas Day – my 12th Christmas. Absolutely unreal. Maybe they'll make me do the whole 33 years and four months . . . no news on my King's Pardon. Could take another three to six months. Was told at the end of September that my pardon was in the palace. I was hoping to be out of here by now. Then again, it could be refused.

CHAPTER 14

THE LAST DAY

A GUARD CAME TO ME and told me I was being released. My King's Pardon, he said, had been approved. I didn't believe him at all. This kind of game was now a popular pastime for the guards and I was not going to disappoint myself again.

Later in the day, however, I had a visit from the missionaries, who confirmed what the guard had told me.

I can't even remember what I felt at this time. I suppose I was never going to believe it.

It was Christmas Day, 1989. I felt as if I had unwrapped a gift, only to find another gift wrapped underneath. I knew that if it were true I would still have to wait.

* * *

On 11 January 1989, a guard opened my cell door and told me to roll up my bed and get my things together. He said I was being released at one o'clock in the afternoon. It was actually happening. Prisoners began coming up to me and saying goodbye. I began to shake like a frightened child. It was so strange. Some of the prisoners hugged me and cried. I felt so sad for them. I knew how horrible it was to see people go, even those you don't know.

* * *

I was walking down the road to the front gate, that same road that I had walked up so many years ago. I saw that nothing had changed. There were the lush gardens and the flies and the stench of the sewage and the rubbish tip. It was as if nothing had happened at all. Bang Kwang was a vacuum in which time came to a stop, while the rest of the world just drifted on by. I turned and looked back at Big Tiger and it was alive. This was a living thing.

I stood with the guards at the gates, waiting for the police who were to escort me away. We talked for a time about strange things – things from the outside world. We were talking like equal people. One of them told me he'd miss me when I was gone. The other told me that when I walked out the gate, I was not to look back at Big Tiger.

'No look back,' he said. 'No look back.'

* * *

The police arrived and I watched as the guard took out the key and opened the massive gates. As he did so, I was struck by the surreal nature of the moment. Here was a human being with the key to my life. At any time, he could have performed this effortless movement and changed the entire shape of my life. A heartbreakingly simple turn of the wrist. The weight and the misery would have been killed in an instant. At any time. The gravity of the thought nearly caused me to faint.

I walked out of Bang Kwang and into the world I hadn't glimpsed for what seemed like a lifetime. The door crashed angrily behind me, as if warning me never to return.

I sat in the police car and he began to drive. I wanted to look back at Big Tiger. I felt it was escaping me too easily, that there was something inside that place I had not resolved.

I looked straight ahead as the car pulled away, following the river that looked so clean and smooth, but ran deep with the bodies of dead things.

CHAPTER 15

HOME

I WAS SUPPOSED TO GO straight to the embassy from the police station, with strict orders to make 'no diversions'. I don't know what they suspected that I might do – after all this, I wasn't likely to make a dash for Chiang Mai to buy heroin. Nevertheless, it seemed I had no choice but to comply. The police drove me to the station where I was to wait for a policeman from the Immigration Department. I was informed that he was not going to arrive until the following day, but this didn't bother me too much. Even this tiny police lock-up, with no bed and no food whatsoever, was the most comfortable place I'd lived in for over a decade.

When the Immigration policeman did arrive in the morning, he had driven me no further than a few hundred yards when a figure on a motorbike sidled up to the driver's window as we were stopped at traffic lights. Some talk ensued which I could not overhear at first, then I realised what was happening. The man at the window was a Thai who I had known in Bang Kwang. He had heard of my release and, knowing the movements of discharged foreign prisoners, had waited for me to come by. He tried to convince the policeman that I did not have to appear at the Immigration holding cell until 8 p.m. that evening, and that I would surely be allowed a little freedom until then. Of course, the policeman was dubious at first, but my friend was very insistent. In the end, the policeman was convinced by that which had converted every enforcement officer I had known: baht. I gave the officer an assurance that I would appear at Immigration that evening, and he drove away.

As I climbed on the back of the motorbike, my friend informed me that his story was rubbish: I did indeed have to appear at Immigration, but he had simply thought I might like to go for something decent to eat beforehand. In any case, what would they do to me now? Throw me back in Bang Kwang? We made our way through the streets of Bangkok, bustling with people as it had years before. These were the streets I had looked upon when Mad Dog held my head over the balcony window, growling into my ear that I'd never be amongst them again. I believed him then, and I suppose, in a sense, he was right: the man on the back of this motorbike was not the man he had uttered those words to. I was momentarily struck with fear as I realised that Mad Dog was probably out here somewhere, waiting for me to stumble right back into his hands. He could then correct the injustice that he saw in my still being alive. It took me a few minutes to wrestle this thought from my head, but it remained lurking in the back of my mind for every moment I remained in the streets of Bangkok.

We arrived at a beautiful restaurant and took a table. In all reality, it was probably a second-rate restaurant, but at this point, any establishment that served more than rice with a fish skeleton was five star to me. I ordered my first beer in nearly 12 years.

A few hours later I began to feel a little anxious about the embassy, and suggested to my friend that perhaps I should at least try to put in an appearance. He seemed to understand my apprehension, so he paid the bill and we left. Upon arrival at the embassy, however, it was lunchtime, and all the relevant officers were unavailable. Being satisfied that I'd made an appearance and done my best, my Thai friend and I made our way back out into

Bangkok in search of a bar. We found one soon enough, where we sat and talked and drank for what seemed an eternity.

It was strange how even the shape of time seemed to change once the walls that had surrounded me for so long had been stripped away. For years now, time had been something of an enemy, the long stretches of boredom and discomfort being serviced by too much thin, dragging time. Now, time was suddenly full again. There were countless things to fill it with, even if I just looked around. A painting on a wall or the colours in a carpet – it was all so nourishing after a world of grey.

Strangely, however, there was very little to talk about for me and my Thai friend. There seemed no point in talking about the prison, yet, naturally, there was little else we knew about. But the long periods of silence were far from uncomfortable. Both of us knew what was happening here. It was a silence of choice. That was good enough.

It was dark as we rode back to Immigration. Winding through a dark backstreet, I cast my eyes upwards and marvelled at what I saw. Stars. I hadn't seen stars in all this time, and there they were, dim from the city lights but brilliant all the same. I recalled that years before I had lain in my cell and dreamed of seeing stars. The night sky was one of the commonplace things I missed while inside the vaults of the prisons. Sometime over the last few years, I'd forgotten that I missed them. Now I remembered, and I wanted to lie back someplace and count every single one. I wondered how many more of these sorts of realisations I would encounter. It would have to end somewhere. My mind would surely overload.

We arrived at Immigration and my friend wished me well. He told me to be careful here as it was a dangerous place. This seemed to me an odd thing to say – after Bang Kwang, how bad could it be? He gave me a look that said so many opposite things: welcome and goodbye; it's been wonderful and terrible; I'm sorry to see you go and I'm glad we'll never see each other again. Then he rode off into the night, my last human connection with the Bangkok prison system.

* * *

The Immigration staff went berserk, shouting at me for explanations as to where I'd been. I said that I thought I hadn't had to be there until 8 p.m., and as far as I was concerned I still had a few minutes left. In any case, I was here now, so what was the problem? I had nowhere else to go.

Apparently, embassy field officers had been scouring the streets of Bangkok, convinced that I'd disappeared into the same criminal labyrinth that had originally landed me in prison. Much later, through a letter from a prisoner, I learned that several officers returned to Bang Kwang, announcing to the guards that they'd lost Warren Fellows. I was told that as news of this filtered through the buildings, Big Tiger went wild.

The situation here seemed quite ridiculous. Although having been visually identified as the man who arrived in the embassy at lunchtime to find nobody but a desk clerk, the Immigration staff treated me like some sort of primary school truant. In an establishment as squeaky clean as this, being told I was a bad boy was like being struck with a feather. Eventually, after fussing around with all sorts of paperwork, the Immigration staff showed me to my cell. It didn't take me long to work out why my friend had warned me of this place.

Immigration was one big room and there were people everywhere, lying all over the floor as we had done in prison. They were filthy and some were obviously sick. The whole place stank. There were guards swaggering around, scowling as they passed the people at their feet. It struck me as a joke – a pretend prison, with fake prisoners and phony guards. All the ingredients of Bang Kwang were there, but it seemed an idle threat. You did not come to this place to spend the rest of your life. You came here on your way home.

There were, however, certain other remarkable similarities between this place and the prisons. When I approached an official with my papers, he informed me that I'd probably be spending at least a few days before a flight could be organised. He then informed me that I was to pay him 400 baht for rental of the floorspace in which I would sleep. The government of Thailand had failed to crush the life out of Warren Fellows, so they were determined to get every last shred of cash out of him as he departed. I informed the official that I simply did not have that amount of money, to which he replied, with the sneer of someone who's about to win a war, that he therefore had no choice but to search me for the money.

That was it. I told him to go and get himself fucked. After all I'd been through there was no way I was going to be intimidated by a bureaucratic mummy's-boy.

In seconds, I was set upon by a large security guard, who began shaping up to throw punches at me. He was tremendously excited, as if he'd been waiting all night for this moment. I was just so fascinated by the fact that this was happening that I don't think I reacted terribly much.

When this stupidity had finally died down, I took my place on the floor and began to count my remaining hours in Thailand. Being patient seemed harder now that there was an end within sight.

I was on a plane bound for Perth, which was the only destination I could afford to get to. I had friends and family there, and the embassy had alerted them to my pending arrival.

The movement of air travel was both familiar and strange. I'd made so many flights in my life, but none in the last eleven-and-a-half years. I'd forgotten the surge and the sway. I began to feel sick. And it was a sickness from which I would not recover for months.

But this was not just a simple case of motion sickness. I think it was the dawning of realisation of what had happened back there in Bangkok – an awareness that showed itself through physical illness. I had been a slave and an animal for a period of time that I could never regain. This was my life, not a dress rehearsal. I'd lost so much. And it was all because I'd climbed onto a machine, just like this one, with a mission that was a mistake. I wondered if this might be the very same plane that I was supposed to board all those years ago. Had things gone differently, I would have been on this plane on 11 October 1978, heading for home and safety. Look what happened instead. I wanted to pick up time and fold it over, so as to cover the years between then and now, but I couldn't. I had to live with this, and I was now aware of the awful possibility that I wouldn't be able to do that.

The girl beside me kept looking at me as if I was an alien creature. I suppose she was right.

* * *

My baggage was thoroughly checked when I went through customs at Perth airport. They found nothing. Nevertheless, two Commonwealth detectives saw fit to pull me aside and usher me into a small room. Reclining in their chairs, and wearing perpetual grins, they proceeded to ask me what, exactly, it was like in Bang Kwang. Though friendly, their interest seemed more voyeuristic than anything else. I didn't mind being asked, but I just didn't know how to sum up the experience of Bangkok. How could I summarise everything I'd seen in one question-and-answer session?

Then one of them asked me a curious question. He pointed to a plant in the corner of the room and asked me if I thought it was real or fake. I can't remember my answer, because I didn't know, but the question scared me. I began to wonder whether anything around me was real, whether my feelings of freedom were true or imagined.

In hindsight, I think they were trying to find out exactly what had been released from Bang Kwang. Was I the right shape for society, or had Bang Kwang simply produced a monster? And I was now beginning to wonder about this myself.

To this day, I still don't know if that plant was real or not.

Eventually, the detectives escorted me out into the main concourse of the airport, where my sister-in-law and nephew were waiting for me.

'Welcome home, Warren,' they whispered as we embraced.

And there was something in those words that just didn't seem quite right.

* * *

At this point in my life, I had catalogued three moments that stood out as the most harrowing: my arrest; my arrival in Maha Chai; my entry to Bang Kwang. I was now beginning to realise that I could add a fourth: coming home.

The day after my arrival in Perth, I made my way to a pub around the corner from the hotel where we were staying. I just wanted to have a few beers alone, to try and get the contents of my head into some sort of order. The previous evening had been full of questions and I didn't know where to start answering. It was all too fast. Everything was too fast. As I sat down with a beer, the strangeness of everything grew louder. I was home in Australia – the place I had dreamed about for so long, during so many stretched black nights in Bang Kwang and Maha Chai and Bumbud and Lard Yao. These were the moments I'd yearned for and they were here, but they were confused and unsettling and numb. I felt as if I didn't want to see anyone, or at least, I didn't want them to see me. Not yet. Just then, I saw a woman walking into the hotel. She had a face more familiar to me than any other face in the world, but one I hadn't seen for so long it seemed unnatural to see it at all. It was my mother.

Just a few days before, she had received a call from the embassy in Bangkok.

'Mrs Fellows, we have some very good news about Warren.'

'Oh, really? How is he going?'

'Mrs Fellows, he was released from prison yesterday. He's on his way home.'

Beside herself with excitement, Mum had flown to Perth and booked a motel room for a week, so that we could sit and talk and get to know each other again. She'd gone to a lot of trouble.

But something terrible was happening to me and it was amplified when she walked into the room. I was now distrustful of my entire situation. For so long, any times of joy were tainted by the knowledge that my captors would soon take such moments away and put an end to the calm. I was worried that the same thing would happen now, that this newfound freedom was just an illusion, and to indulge in it was too dangerous.

So, when my mother approached, I just snapped at her. Before I even said as much as hello, I accused her of following me and told her to go away and let me be. Mum was crying and trying to hold me but I was recoiling, rejecting my own emotions. I felt like I had to reject hers as well. For the sanity of both of us. Some part of me knew I was glad to see her, but I was troubled too. I didn't know how to react or behave. We'd both been through so much. My ordeal is this story, which you have read. Hers is another entirely. The last time she'd been to Perth was for Gary's funeral. One year later, Dad died. And, in the middle of all of this, the knowledge – which must have been unbearable for her – that her son was being held in a tortuous situation, at the hands of strangers far away. I had heard that, during the whole time I was in Bangkok, she never went outside the house for Mother's Day. That seemed so sad to me. I was crushed by a deep sense of responsibility to her, and I just did not know how to cope. All I can say today is that, at the moment when we re-entered each other's lives, I was unprepared for the shock, in every way.

* * *

Almost as soon as we arrived at the motel, I lay down on the bed and drifted into some kind of emotional coma. I became delirious, waking every now and then wondering which world I was in. My mother became concerned enough to dress me and take me to a hospital. The doctors reported that I was dreadfully undernourished and that I had also contracted pneumonia. They suggested that the best thing to do would be to get me home to Sydney as soon as possible.

My mother had not planned to return so early. One nurse from the hospital, aware of the entire story regarding myself and my mother, offered to pay both our airfares home. Mum was staggered by the kindness but could not accept.

'Thank you so much,' she told the nurse, 'but we'll be all right. I'll get Warren home somehow.'

* * *

I awoke in Sydney, completely unaware that I had just crossed the breadth of the country. I was disorientated and frightened by how I was feeling. It was as if being this way had been tolerable in jail – almost appropriate – but here, surrounded by the comforts of the real world, it was too harsh. I felt desperately weak and like I couldn't bear to touch anything.

Wandering out into the living-room of my mother's apartment, I saw her sitting there on the couch and felt a sudden need to apologise.

'I'm sorry,' I kept repeating, 'but I don't know what's the matter with me. I don't know what's the matter.'

After a few days, Mum took me to a hospital in Sydney, where I would remain for two weeks. During this time, I began to get used to the idea that people actually do care for you when you are sick. These are the simple human things that I would have to re-educate myself about. It was like being a newborn baby, only everyone expected me to react like an adult of the world. I must have seemed like a spoilt, mute child.

A further fly in the ointment was the sudden onslaught of reporters. Keen to get the first exclusive interview, they began to besiege the hospital. Worst of all was Mike Munro, who managed to gain entry to my ward and attempted to secure an interview while I was hooked up to an oxygen mask. My mother begged him several times to leave us be, but Mike wouldn't have it, acting with a kind of disgust at the fact that I was denying the public something that they truly deserved. He managed to force my mother to become as hostile as she'd ever been in her life. After all she'd been through – death, tragedy, untold heartache – it was a thing called Mike Munro that finally caused her to lose her temper.

I don't care if they're 'just doing their jobs', any more than I care that Mad Dog or Prisit were doing theirs.

* * *

It took me some weeks to be able to socialise at all. My first night out was a dinner party arranged by old friends – now quite new friends, of course.

When we arrived at the chosen venue, I was astonished to see that it was a Chinese restaurant, with a big golden dragon painted on the window. As my brain did a rebound from this image, my friends were laughing.

'We thought you might like some fried rice,' one of them roared.

I pretended to laugh with them, but deep down I was heartbroken. I cannot blame them for this, and I know that it was easier for me to understand their joke than it would have been for them to understand my sense of shock. But that was the very point. From this moment forward, I realised the tremendous distance that would forever stand between myself and the others. Nobody would ever know where I'd been. They could imagine it well enough, and I know that most of them tried as best they could. But really, as far as they were concerned, I'd just been away, and now I was back. It was time for me to be happy and get on with my life. To forget the past.

But I couldn't forget the past, not when it had changed me so ruthlessly. Every time I looked in the mirror or saw something commonplace that I hadn't seen for years, I was reminded of what a different world I was now from, and how different I had become because of it. Everything around me seemed to buzz with strangeness. Life was just as misshapen and unfamiliar as it had been when I first entered Bumbud.

I couldn't make people understand – I didn't even feel that I wanted to – so I had to conform to their lack of understanding. That sort of thinking puts a wall between yourself and the rest of the world. A prison.

* * *

I went for a walk in the streets where my mother lived, and I saw that people even looked different. The whole punk thing had happened while I'd been inside and kids were now walking around with orange hair and shocking symbols on their T-shirts. It seemed the whole world had grown up and become extroverted, while I'd been in a training camp for introverts. For all the time in Bangkok, I'd become used to having to do everything in secret. But here, in the world, people had become so wide-open about things, particularly drugs. One night in a pub, I noticed people taking Ecstasy, handing it out right there in the middle of the room, in plain view of everyone. I couldn't believe it. It was as if the laws that had confined me for all this time had been abolished in my absence. I remember feeling that I had more in common with the inmates of Bang Kwang than the regulars of this pub.

On that same night, I left my coat hanging over a chair as I went to the bar to buy a drink. When I returned, I reached into the pocket and found that something was missing – my address book. In it were the names and addresses of everyone from Bang Kwang who I had wanted to stay in touch with. Everything happens for a reason, and I suppose losing this book might have been a good thing – I now had no link to my awful experience in Thailand. But I couldn't control this weird feeling that, once again, someone was trying to separate me from my family.

* * *

Eventually, I caught up with Paul. It was fantastic to see him, despite the obvious strangeness of seeing him in a place like a pub. I'd become so used to seeing his face against a grey background. His mood seemed a little sombre, but at the time I put that down to the same feelings that were making life difficult for myself.

I was fascinated when Paul told me what had become of Neddy Smith. I had always known that he was a serious underworld contender, or at least on his way there, but I never expected him to take on some kind of Ned Kelly status. The tales were full of violence and merciless greed, and that is not the Neddy I knew. Prior to speaking to Paul on this occasion, I had never heard of Roger Rogerson, though I believe he was already making an appearance in Ned's life when Paul and I were arrested. I have not seen Ned since leaving Australia in 1978 and, to this day, we've never spoken of what happened all those years ago. There's not much to say.

Paul himself had a sad story to tell. His daughter, Kelly, had stopped speaking when he was arrested. For months she refused to say a word, until one day her dentist held up a picture of Paul that he had obtained somehow.

'Daddy,' Kelly cried instantly.

Now, said Paul, she had grown up into a young woman, and had trouble acknowledging who he was. His second daughter, Belinda, had no idea who he was at all. Paul was obviously struggling as he told me this.

Over my next few meetings with Paul, it became apparent that his peculiar emotional state was not just a flash in the pan. Paul was not adjusting to freedom at all. He constantly lapsed into thinking he was back there, dreaming up ways of survival. It became clear to me that Paul was falling into a void from which he might not escape.

From what I could gather, he had been the centre of attention for a time after he resumed, with all sorts of distant acquaintances struggling to get an audience with him. After the initial novelty had worn off, however, Paul had found himself very much alone. He had a family, of course, who cared for him greatly, but they had also grown up without him. He couldn't make peace with that reality. There was no way for him to 'forget the past' and simply 'get on with his life', for he had been unlucky enough to contract HIV and tuberculosis while in prison. In essence, Paul Hayward had never been released from Bang Kwang.

I do think that had they not separated Paul and me in Bang Kwang, we'd both be all right today. Together, we somehow managed to share the misery and balance it out, as if we were on a seesaw. We'd come into this thing together and, right from that stupid failed suicide pact in the police lock-up in Bangkok, we were determined to tough it out together. But that bond disintegrated when Paul was taken away. Suddenly, we both had to run our own race. Paul was an extremely capable man, but he was also deeply sensitive. This was one contest he just couldn't win without his team.

In the winter of 1992, Paul Hayward died of a heroin overdose. Whether this was his intention or not, I don't really know for sure. It doesn't matter. To make such a mistake would seem to indicate a certain loss of will to survive, particularly in such a natural survivor as Paul.

All I can say for sure is that I miss him as much as I miss anyone who ever lived in this world.

* * *

I have a dream where Paul is trying to tell me something. There is a wire fence dividing us and I know that he is on the outside. He beckons me to come closer. He is whispering a warning that I cannot hear. His face is soft but concerned. I can see his mouth moving but there are no words. I approach the fence to be nearer to him, to hear what he is so desperately trying to tell me, but he turns and begins to walk away. And I call out to him until he is gone.

* * *

One night, as I was drinking with friends in a hotel, a man approached me and, talking over my shoulder, inquired as to whether I had known his brother. I turned and looked at him. He was a thick-set, dark-skinned man who I didn't recognise. I replied that I did not know his brother, turned and continued to drink with my friends. Without warning, the man's fist came crashing against the side of my face, dropping me from my chair and breaking my jaw in three places. I spent the next six weeks with my jaw wired, all the while trying to figure out who it could have been and why he had wanted to break me in two.

After a time, I returned to the hotel in the hope of seeing the man. I didn't want to retaliate against him – I simply wanted to find out what his story was. Perhaps, I thought, he had a brother who had been in prison with me, or someone who had somehow been involved in the sordid business that took place before I left for Bangkok. There was also the depressing possibility that his brother had been a heroin addict, and this man was one of the many who might want to take their revenge on Warren Fellows.

I wasn't there for long before another man approached me and offered his hand. He was the brother of the man who had struck me and he wanted to apologise. His brother, he said, had simply been having a bad night. As it turned out, he'd had nothing against me personally, and was simply reacting on a violent impulse he couldn't explain or understand.

Can people sense that a person has lived in a violent environment, and therefore is an attractor for violence? I wonder, but I hope not. Today, I can't stomach the sight of violence. There was so much of it all around me for so long, always a product of the fear, desperation and cruelty that made up our world. I can no longer understand why anybody who lives in a free, comfortable society would want to create a violent situation. Sometimes, I can't even look at a violent film. That wicked look on a man's face when he is trying to destroy another's life, and the look of terror on the face of the victim – I can't bear to look at those faces. For nearly 12 years they were the faces that were all around me. Those expressions symbolise my life in that place and I never want to see them again.

In a way, faces were all I ever had to look at. When all you have is walls and faces, the faces are what you concentrate on. Every detail of every expression becomes a significant detail of your life. I've become acutely aware of changes in facial expressions and their hidden meanings. In Bangkok, a person's face could tell you so much. In a lot of ways, it was the only method of communication we had. A blink of an eye or a twist of the lip could tell you a story. 'So-and-so has the stuff you want' or 'so-and-so plans to kill you tonight' – these messages were all sent with such symbols. These days, a person in my company will do something completely natural, like scratch their cheek or their nose, and for a moment I'll think they are trying to tell me something. Those signals used to mean the difference between life and death. My awareness is still heightened, perhaps too much for normal society. I can hear things that people say on the other side of a room, and all my reflexes and shields kick into gear. It can be very disturbing, but it can also play in my favour.

I'm aware that I am a curiosity to some people. I'll meet someone who appears not to know who I am, and that's the way I like it. But, so often, it doesn't take long for the façade to fall. The person will begin asking me what I have been doing for the last decade or so.

It becomes obvious that they know, and then the quiz show begins. I just have to weather the storm.

While I can understand this sort of curiosity, I can't understand why people want to play games with me so often. They begin with simple questions, then, as the night progresses and they realise I'm not going to maul them like an animal, they start to push it, saying deliberately offensive things or invading my personal space. It's as if they want to prove to themselves that they can match wit and muscle with a notorious criminal. They can go home to their leafy terrace houses and bask in the knowledge that they can cut it with the baddies.

But they're stupid if they think I don't realise this. For all the time I was incarcerated, I had nothing to do but survive from day to day. That was my job. In order to do this, I had to outfox a system that was fully prepared for me to try and outfox it. I had to manipulate minds that were on their guard. My own mind is a mess in so many ways, but it still has the power to do this. I've had 12 years of training in reading minds and using my own to slip out of the grasp of others. While most people I meet have spent that time living with the world – focusing on work, on relationships, on movies or television or sport or a million other distractions – I've been forced to concentrate solely on surviving mental siege. If somebody wants to play a mind game with me, they'd better be as good as Prisit. Otherwise, they will lose, and they probably won't even realise they have.

Just recently, someone said to me: 'Come on, Warren. You're free now.' But I'm not, really. Three-quarters of my mind is always there.

I'll hear a flag fluttering and think of the flags on the walls of Bang Kwang. I might see a crowd of children coming home from school, and I think of how much life they've got ahead of them and how much I've lost. All I ever seem to do is think and think and think.

After reading the last few pages, you might now believe that I'm just wallowing in self-pity, and, well, I am. Of course I feel sorry for myself. More correctly, I feel sorry to myself. How could I not? I'd have a head made of stone if I didn't. It's because I pity myself so much that I don't feel the need to ask for pity from anyone else.

And, of course, there are those of you who feel that I should spend more time feeling sorry for the people that I hurt by being a drug merchant – those whose lives were ruined by drugs. I do feel sorry for them, for in what surely is an outstanding case of poetic justice, I became one of them too. I know what a wreck life can be when drugs take a hold. I think I probably feel more pity for them than a person who has never been addicted to drugs could feel.

Now that I've got my heart back, it is a bottomless pit of sorrow and pity. There's plenty to go around. Oh, God, sometimes I wish they had just taken a gun and shot me through the heart.

* * *

That was a frustrated curse. I don't really wish that at all. It was just a thought I had yesterday and today I don't feel so bad. There are many things I can do. It's sunny outside and I'm going to help my mother pick up a new washing machine for the apartment.

EPILOGUE

TOWARDS THE END OF 1996, a man phoned me and asked me for help. He said that his wife had just been arrested in Thailand for heroin trafficking. A journalist had told him I might be able to help. Except for a few lame words of assurance there was no help I could give.

Several months later, his wife appeared on the news, sentenced to 50 years. My feelings were scrambled. I was appalled for her and her husband. I must say, though, that I was also relieved it was someone else and not me. I thought of the long years ahead for her, and how awful it would be to be back there again, right at the very beginning. I find it hard to fit into society, but at least I'm not back there. I'll never be there again.

If there is one thing that I sincerely hope my story has brought to you, it is the wisdom that I did not have before I began my journey. I now know that there is nothing more precious than a free life. No amount of money is worth the risk I took. No amount in the world.

While working on this book, I was in a bar in the city when I overheard a young, fresh-faced girl telling a friend of an offer she had been made: to bring some hashish back from Indonesia, for a fee of $5,000. I listened to her talk for a while, comparing her innocence to everything I'd experienced in Thailand. I thought of that Thai prisoner, clinging to the fence as he was dragged toward the last minute of his life, desperately clutching for a few more seconds. Those seconds – the very seconds that would make up this young girl's life – are worth more than a miserable $5,000. More than five billion. They're priceless.

Some say that people cannot be warned, that they have to experience things for themselves before they learn. I know there is some truth in that. But if my recollection of the horrors I experienced can change the mind of one person, then my loss has not been worthless. It will, in fact, become as priceless as a life.

* * *

There is another dream that I have perhaps every year or so. I am sitting on a beach, late in the afternoon. I am with two young women, one on either side of me. We are talking and laughing and the scene is completely innocent and natural – as natural as it used to be for me before I went away. As the sun begins to fade, they suggest that we go someplace for dinner, then perhaps out for a night on the town. In an instant, I feel a warm wave of relief wash over me, as if the strangeness of my life, the blackness that covers everything, has been lifted. I can be a normal human being. I can fit in. The world is exciting and young and there is a good life to be had after all.

Suddenly, I hear a familiar rattling sound. I turn to see the guard standing there, the keys to the cells dangling from his hand. The girls have disappeared. It's time to go, says the guard. And he calls me by my name.

I awake from this dream and take a few minutes to get myself together, unsure as to whether I'm home or in that place. I'll go out into the kitchen and make myself a cup of coffee. Or tea. Having that choice is something.

I'll spend the rest of the day convincing myself that I'm not in that place any more. But I know that place, the horrors that occurred, and all the loss it delivered me is buried in my heart forever.

And from that, I'm afraid, I can't ever be free.

APPENDIX

Standard Minimum Rules for the Treatment of Prisoners
(Adopted by the First United Nations Congress on the Prevention of
Crime and the Treatment of Offenders on August 30 1955 and approved
by the United Nations Economic and Social Council on July 31 1957)

Article 31
Corporal punishment, punishment by placing in a dark cell, and all cruel,
inhumane or degrading punishments shall be completely prohibited as
punishments for disciplinary offences.

Article 32
(1) Punishment by close confinement or reduction of diet shall never be
inflicted unless the medical officer has examined the prisoner and certified
in writing that he is fit to sustain it.
(2) The same shall apply to any other punishment that may be prejudicial
to the physical or mental health of the prisoner. In no case may such
punishment be contrary to or depart from the principle stated in Rule 31.
(3) The medical officer shall visit daily prisoners undergoing such
punishments and shall advise the director if he considers the termination
or alteration of the punishment necessary on the grounds of physical or
mental health.

Article 33
Instruments of restraint, such as handcuffs, chains, irons and straitjackets
shall never be applied as a punishment. Furthermore, chains or irons shall
not be used as restraints . . .